# Moments with Children in Worship

# MOMENTS WITH CHILDREN IN WORSHIP

## THROUGH THE CHURCH YEAR

edited by Joseph H. Bragg, Jr.

CBP Press

St. Louis, Missouri

**Library of Congress Cataloging-in-Publication Data**

Moments with children in worship / edited by Joseph H. Bragg Jr.

    144 p.   cm.
    Includes index.
    ISBN 0-8272-2320-X
    1. Children's sermons.  I. Bragg, Joseph H.
BV4315. M59 1989
252'.53—dc19                          88–27590

                                                CIP

*Printed in the United States of America*

# Contents

# Introduction

*Joseph H. Bragg, Jr.*

Worship is at the very heart of the church. Within worship the congregation both discovers and expresses its focus, and from worship the congregation derives its strength and direction.

As the community of faith, persons of all ages come together in worship to declare that they belong to God through Jesus Christ. Through hymns and prayers they praise, confess, and petition. They confront the Word through Scripture and sermon. They experience renewal around the sacred table. Every aspect of the service is designed to lift the worshipers into a sense of oneness with each other and with God.

Into this corporate experience come our children. What shall we do with them? How shall we involve them? Years ago, no one worried about that. Children were part of the whole. They participated where and when they could, and no one was bothered by an occasional disturbance.

Today we feel the need to do something special. In recent years, that "something special" in many churches has been the children's sermon or children's moment. The children come to the front of the sanctuary in the middle of the worship service. They share a brief moment with the pastor, associate pastor, or some other adult. For both the children and the onlooking worshipers, the time may be entertaining, sweet, and amusing.

The problem is that the children's sermon frequently has little, if anything, to do with worship. Too often the worshipers become an audience—spectators to a scene about which they may smile or chuckle, exclaim, "Aren't they cute?", and generally feel good. The "presider" becomes a stand-up comic, or the clever fielder of children's questions and comments, or the teller of nice moralisms the adults want their children to hear. And the children become attention-getting entertainers, pleased with their central position in the scene but void of any understanding of the meaning of the moment. And where is God, object of all worship? No doubt looking on with kind amusement and patience.

So what shall we do with this children's sermon or children's moment? If there is to be some special time when the children come to the front of the sanctuary, then the time must be planned in a way that enhances the worship experience of all. The focus must be on the same qualities of the Christian faith and life that are expressed and experienced in other parts of the service of worship. The intellectual and emotional energy must move toward God, just as it must in all other parts of this central act of the faith community. The participants must be recognized as those same persons who sing and pray and listen and commune. There are no spectators and no entertainers; there are only worshipers.

The selections in this book were written by people who are serious about worship and who are convinced of the importance of full participation of children in the worship of the congregation. They recognize that worship is both an intellectual and an emotional activity and that the Spirit moves amidst the process to bind the community to one another and to God. These selections are called sermons because they blend scripture with contemporary words in the hope that they may become the Word for those who see and hear and share. They are not rigid purveyors of truth, but carriers of opportunities for recognizing the moment of revelation as a unique mixture of the Spirit and the personalities of all who share in the experience. Finally, these selections are viewed as an integral part of worship.

The purpose of this book is to provide suggestions to those responsible for leading moments with children in worship. The eight writers come to their task from different backgrounds and perspectives and with entirely different styles. And that is good. It is important for all leaders of worship to function within their own styles and personalities. Readers will want to adapt these selections to meet the needs of their own congregations and their own unique way of leading worship.

The book is organized around the church year, beginning with Advent and Christmas and moving through Epiphany, Lent, Easter, and Pentecost. Sermons for the first seasons focus on Jesus Christ, climaxing in his resurrection. Lent does, however, use some teachings of Jesus regarding the Christian life. The season of Easter emphasizes God's love and forgiveness, the love within families, and the special gifts of people.

The second half of the church year is the season of Pentecost. After seven sermons on Pentecost and the church, this section includes emphases on discipleship, creation, and special days.

The church year provides a framework through which the worship services of the congregation comprehensively embrace the whole life of Jesus Christ and the church that calls him Lord. It gives flow and organization to this central part of the church's life.

Within the framework of the church year, this book offers suggestions for special emphases that occur in the lives of many congregations. Within the season of Epiphany, there is one selection for use on Martin Luther King, Jr. Sunday and one that can be used during the Week of Prayer for Christian Unity. The season of Easter includes a selection that is appropriate for Mother's Day or Family Week. "The More We Get Together," one of the Pentecost sermons, emphasizes oneness in Christ and is appropriate for World Communion Sunday. The section on discipleship, also in Pentecost, includes two sermons on stewardship that can be used on Pledge Sunday or during a congregation's financial drive. Two sermons on growing and learning are in that same section for possible use at the beginning of the church school year. The final section within the season of Pentecost offers suggestions for four special days that occur in the fall.

An index of scripture references at the back of the book indicates sermons based on specific passages. Use it as a way of coordinating these special moments with children with the lectionary or the themes of particular worship services.

It is hoped that this book will serve as a resource that has both direction and flexibility. The intent is that it be used, not in any special order nor as the source of canned presentation, but as a stimulus for creatively involving all worshipers in praise to God and for intentionally planning moments with children in worship that are integral parts of a whole and holy experience.

# Introduction to Advent/ Christmas

## R. Larry Hallett

Advent is a time of beginnings and waiting—beginning the church year and waiting expectantly for the birth of Christ. "Waiting" is the theme of the season. "Expectantly" is its style, its feeling. Our task as Christian educators at this joyous time is just that: to bring to bear the joy that is inherent in our gathering as a church family to wait. And not just to wait passively and have something done for us or to us. We wait *expectantly*, which means that *we* do something. We anticipate. We prepare. We make ready. We give. And then we receive far greater than we could ever deserve.

The overall purpose of this section is, of course, to prepare the children *and* the church for the coming of the Christ Child. This preparation takes place both individually and corporately. Now, perhaps more than ever, children should be as involved as possible in the sharing of the story, the story we call Christmas.

One common way to accomplish this involvement is with the lighting of the Advent wreath. Allowing a child or group of children—under adult supervision and with appropriate explanation—to be included in one of the weeks of lighting is a good experience for everyone.

Another exciting possibility is to encourage the children to arrange the crèche or manger scene. Each week the figures are advanced further toward the stable, or additional figures are added each week to build the crèche. All effort should be made throughout Advent to heighten anticipation and awareness within the child of the joy we share as a church family in the self-giving of God through Christ.

A third option would be to read various Christmas stories or to incorporate these stories of Christmas into the sermon. Many so-called nonreligious or secular stories that deal with Christmas often drive home the point of selfless giving in profoundly moving ways. Christmas *is* a story; try to capture and maintain that same narrative mode in your sermons.

Christmas is a time of multiple sense sensations: taste, smell, sight, hearing, touch. All come into play daily during the Advent season (e.g. smell: holly, candles; taste: treats, perhaps from other countries; touch: holding hands). Use these to your advantage whenever possible.

When we build this anticipatory wait carefully and thoroughly, we prepare our children not only for the hope, peace, love, and joy at Christmas, but we help lay the foundation for the entire liturgical year. *Emmanuel: God with us!* That's our good news to relate. Spread the joy!

# Waiting and Hoping
## (First Sunday of Advent)

**Purpose:** To help the children wait for Christmas with thoughts of the birth of Jesus.
**Scripture:** Matthew 1:18–21a.
**Materials:** An alarm clock or food timer.

**Sermon:** *[Begin by setting the alarm clock or timer for approximately 5-7 minutes, depending on the length of the message. The clock is to develop anticipation and waiting. Make it very obvious. Then read the scripture.]*
Let's talk about hope for a bit. We all know what hope is, don't we? What is hope? *[Take a short time to field answers.]*
Those are all good responses, and now I want to share another idea of hope. This is Advent. The word "Advent" means "coming." It's a time of waiting and preparing for God's coming—in the form of a baby in a manger. When we wait and prepare for someone, what do we do? Pretend that someone extra special is coming for a visit. What would you do to prepare for his or her visit? *[Again, allow time for responses.]*
One thing we might do would be to clean up the house or maybe decorate it nicely, just as we are going to decorate the church today (*or next week*). We might bake some cookies or wrap a nice gift for that favorite person. When it gets time for our special friend to arrive, we would probably get really excited and stand by the window or door—waiting, watching, hoping that they would come *real soon!*
That's what Advent is all about—preparing, waiting, watching, and hoping. Preparing for the coming of God in Jesus. Waiting for the time to arrive. Watching for signs, like clocks or calendars or stars, that tell us something is happening.
And hoping for many things to happen, like gifts and hugs, stories and love being shared. The feeling is sort of like watching the clock and waiting for the alarm to go off. Tick,

tock. We can hear the time passing, and we know the alarm will go off soon. We're waiting and watching and hoping and waiting and . . . *[If the timing is right, the alarm or timer should go off about now. You'll have to experiment with timing to ensure greater success, especially with the two open-question periods earlier.]*

There it is! After the waiting and watching and hoping, it happened.

Advent is a time when we wait and watch and hope. We *know* Christmas will be here soon, when we will celebrate the birth of Jesus. It's exciting to wait and hope for Christmas, isn't it?

**Prayer:** Thank you, dear God, for this happy, exciting, wonderful time of Advent once again. May we wait for the coming of baby Jesus into our lives with joy, peace, love, and above all, hope. Amen.

# Jesus Is the Name
## (Second Sunday of Advent)

**Purpose:** To convey the total sense of joyful enthusiasm we have as we eagerly approach the birth of Jesus.
**Scripture:** Luke 1:26–33.
**Materials:** A medium-sized stick and a stone.

**Sermon:** *[Read scripture.]*
How many of you have ever heard this little rhyme before?

Sticks and stones may break my bones,
but words will never hurt me.

Looks as if almost all of us know that one. What does it mean? *[Wait briefly for responses.]* That's right. Sticks and stones can hurt us. That's why I brought along these "samples" today. We know that if someone hits with this stick or throws this stone really hard it will *hurt!* That's why we always try to be careful with hard things like these, don't we? So we don't hurt ourselves or someone else.

What about the other part of the rhyme: "Words will never hurt me"? What does that mean? Very good; that's right. If someone calls us a name, we want to try not to let ourselves feel hurt or upset by that. Because we *know* that we are not those mean things they might be calling us. God loves us, and we need to love ourselves.

But words or names don't have to be mean. They can be nice names. Wonderful names. What happened in the Bible reading this morning? An angel visited Mary and told her she was going to have a baby. Do you remember what the angel called Mary? "O favored one." That means God had chosen her to do something special.

And what was the name that Mary was to call the baby Jesus? The name Jesus comes from a Hebrew word that means "God saves." God saves us through Jesus. What other names would the baby Jesus be called? Son of God, Wonder-

14

ful Counselor, Prince of Peace, Emmanuel (which means "God with us").

These people and the angels just couldn't help calling people names! They were so excited! But the names chosen were good names, nice names. Jesus was a very special name for a very special person.

**Prayer:** Eternal God, bring us today your special message of peace: That Jesus is our Savior, our Prince of Peace. May we find hope, peace, love, and joy in his name. Amen.

# Songs of Love
## (Third Sunday of Advent)

**Purpose:** To help the children view our Christmas carols as songs of our love of God.

**Scripture:** Luke 1:46–55 (The Magnificat).

**Materials:** Cassette recorder and classical Christmas music.

**Sermon:** *[Begin by reading scripture, abbreviated, if desired, to Luke 1:46–49.]*

Today is the third Sunday of Advent, and we lit the candle of love this morning. Now we all know about love, don't we? Tell me someone you love. *[Take time for discussion/responses.]*

What do you do when you love someone? How do you show them that you love them? *[Again, wait for brief response.]*

Those are all good ideas. Usually when I want to show someone how much I love them, I try to do something extra nice for him or her. Like getting that person a drink when he or she wants one, sending him or her a pretty card for a birthday, helping him or her with a difficult job—things like that.

How does God show love for us? *[Talk about God's many gifts, blessings, etc.—greatest gift being Jesus.]*

God's greatest gift to us—because God loves us so very much—was to send a small baby to us who was Jesus. God showed us love by giving us something *very* special.

God also showed great love by being with Mary and Joseph, by sending angels as messengers, and by guiding the shepherds and wise men to find the baby Jesus.

Remember our scripture reading this morning? How did Mary show her love for God? She sang a song of praise to God. That was the best way that Mary could think of to thank God for blessing her life. She sang a song to God. I think that's really nice, don't you?

16

I've played some music for you while we've talked so you could hear other songs that people have used to praise God at Christmastime. And this morning, as our choir sings, we'll know that we, too, can offer our love and thanks to God in song. That's what our Christmas carols are, aren't they? Songs of our love of God.

**Prayer:** Loving God, may our songs today overflow with praise to you, as Mary's did so long ago. Help us, dear God, to find new ways to feel your love for us and to show our love for you, for ourselves, and for others. Amen.

# An Exciting Announcement
## (Fourth Sunday of Advent)

**Purpose:** To help the children feel the excitement of the birth of Jesus.

**Scripture:** Isaiah 9:6; Luke 2:8–14.

**Materials:** Choose one of the following: birth announcements, pencils engraved with an appropriate message announcing a birth, a similar symbol that announces a birth.

**Sermon:** *[Begin by reading scripture.]*

How many of you have little brothers or sisters? Do you remember when they were born? Did you go to the hospital to see your brother or sister?

What usually happens after a new baby is born? One very important thing that new mommies and daddies want to do is tell other people about it. How many of you that have little brothers or sisters remember telling someone about the new baby?

When we do that, we call that a birth announcement. We are announcing that a new baby has been born. And we can announce a birth in many ways.

Sometimes we put a little notice in the newspaper, like this. *[Have a sample, if possible.]*

Sometimes we hand out formal birth announcements like these.

Or maybe we just send little cards to everyone we know.

People today might give a pencil with the baby's name on it. That makes a really useful gift, doesn't it?

The scripture that I read this morning talks about the announcement of Jesus' birth by an angel to the shepherds in the field. God was so excited about the coming of Jesus that an angel was sent by God to be a messenger, to tell others about Jesus' birth.

Wow! What an announcement! No newspapers or pencils or cards. An angel! No wonder the shepherds were surprised and kind of frightened. They weren't used to having angels visit them. But an angel told them: Don't be afraid. God loves you and has been gracious—very good—to you. For a baby has been born, who is your Savior.

God was bringing a very special baby into the world. God wanted everyone—especially these shepherds watching their flocks—to know just how special the baby was going to be. So God sent out a birth announcement by way of an angel. God loves us very much!

**Prayer:** Joyous God, fill us with your enthusiasm and excitement, so that we may overflow with joy and be messengers of the good news. Amen.

# A Special Gift
## (Christmas Day)

**Purpose:** To acknowledge the birth of Christ. To receive God's great gift.

**Scripture:** Luke 2:1–20.

**Materials:** A large box wrapped half in Christmas wrap and half in a bright birthday wrap; a large candle if there is no Christ candle with the Advent wreath.

**Sermon:** *[Light Christ candle and read scripture.]*

Good morning! There's no need to tell you all what this is. I'm sure you received some brightly colored packages just like this one a little earlier today. It's nice and a lot of fun to receive gifts at Christmastime, isn't it? I hope we all remembered to say "Thank you" for those wonderful gifts.

I want *you* to help me now with this present. Anybody notice anything different about it? That's right. It's wrapped with two kinds of paper. Why do you suppose I did that? *[Take a few minutes to field responses.]* That's correct, again. Half of it is wrapped in Christmas paper because it is Christmas Day. And half of it is wrapped in birthday paper to remind us that it is Jesus' birthday that we are celebrating.

Now let's open it. *[Encourage children to assist in the tearing of the wrap and the opening of the box; save wrap for future use.]* See what is inside? A Nativity scene. Sometimes we call that a créche.

Okay. This is where you really come in. I'm going to lift out a figure, and I want you to tell me about it—who or what it is, what it does in our Christmas story, things like that. *[Take out pieces, one at a time, in whatever order is preferred. Ask different children about each figure until you have developed the créche and completed the story as highlighted by scripture and explained by the children. Special note: Leave wise men in box until following Sunday.]*

Very good! That was nice and fun, too. One last thing: What did the shepherds do as they were leaving? They praised God for what they had seen and been given. That means they thanked God for this wonderful gift, for giving us Jesus. Let's do that now together, in prayer.

**Prayer:** Great and wonderful God, we thank you today for the gift that we have all received, your son Jesus. You gave us the Christ Child because you love us and we love you. Amen.

# The Wise Men
## (First Sunday After Christmas)

**Purpose:** To help the children reflect on the special gift God gave us in Jesus.
**Scripture:** Matthew 2:1-2, 7-11.
**Materials:** Créche.

**Sermon:** *[Read scripture.]*
Several weeks ago, on the first Sunday in Advent, we talked about waiting for Christmas and watching for a friend to arrive. We've talked about Advent and Mary and Joseph and shepherds and angels. On Christmas, just a few days ago, we opened a package that I had brought here for all of you to share.

If you weren't here then, that package had this nativity scene in it, and we talked about and arranged each of the figures as we took them out of the box. We recreated the Christmas story and built our own manger scene.

But a few figures aren't here. This créche is not quite complete. Anybody have any good ideas as to what might be missing?

Very good. The wise men, about whom we just read, are missing. *[Bring out these remaining figures and place them appropriately.]*These were wise men that came from faraway places, traveled a great distance, to bring gifts to the baby Jesus. They had seen a star, which led them to Bethlehem and to the stable. And they knew that this baby was *very* special.

Remember what they brought as gifts? Gold, frankincense, and myrrh. You all know what gold is, right? Good. The other gifts, frankincense and myrrh, were used like incense and perfume. They smelled very good.

What types of gifts would we bring today to a very new and special baby? *[Field responses.]*

These are all good ideas you have. We, like the wise men, would bring gifts that we think are useful and nice or that the

22

baby might need and enjoy later. And we, like the wise men, would bring those gifts out of love, because we really wanted to.

Today, I want to give you a small gift, although you might not think it is a gift. Here is a piece of the wrapping paper from our package last week, on Christmas Day, when we unwrapped our nativity scene and created our very own Christmas story. It doesn't matter whether it's Christmas wrap or birthday wrap. In fact, you can trade with someone if you wish.

What is important is that you remember this package whenever you look at the piece of wrapping paper. I want you to remember what was inside—the manger scene and the baby Jesus—God's most precious gift ever to all of us. And even if you happen to lose this little piece of wrap, don't worry. The paper may be lost, but God doesn't get lost. God is always going to be with us.

**Prayer:** Dearest God, after a hopeful, peace-filled, loving, and joyous Christmas, help us to know that your love remains and that you are always with us, Emmanuel. Amen.

# Introduction to Epiphany

## Janet Hellner-Burris

The season of Epiphany seems rather quiet after the joyous pageants, parties, caroling, and gift-giving of the Advent season and Christmas Day. Yet in many countries the feasting and exchange of gifts associated with Christmas take place on Epiphany—on the day when the wise men found the newborn King and honored him with their strange and exotic gifts of gold, frankincense, and myrrh. January 6 is the day of Epiphany. In our ecumenical lectionary, it is celebrated on the Sunday between January 2 and January 8.

Though the celebration of Epiphany has been forgotten in much of the English-speaking world, Epiphany is making a comeback in many congregations. What better time to teach children the real meaning of Christ's birth than on Epiphany Sunday, after all the secular influences surrounding Christmas have faded away?

This series of children's sermons begins with the celebration of Epiphany and continues with the early ministry of Jesus, his baptism, temptations, and the calling of the twelve disciples. It includes the parables of the two home builders and the good Samaritan, and two texts from the Sermon on the Mount: "Where your treasure is" and "Judge not." There are two special children's sermons created for observing Martin Luther King, Jr. Sunday and the Week of Prayer for Christian Unity.

# On Giving Gifts

**Purpose:** To remind children and the congregation about the story of Epiphany. To stress the need to give gifts to Jesus, not just to each other, during the Christmas season.
**Scripture:** Matthew 2:1–12.
**Materials:** A manger scene with all of the figures in it except the wise men, who are hidden not far from the children. A few weeks ahead of Epiphany, invite each church school class or all church members and families to bring a gift for Jesus on Epiphany Sunday. Some suggestions for gifts might include pledges to serve a meal to the homeless, visit a shut-in, give additional money to missions, pray for peace every day. Each present should be wrapped, and someone should be selected to present the gift in worship.

**Sermon:** I brought from home the manger scene I use during the Christmas season. Can you tell me the names and a little bit about each figure? *[Mary, Joseph, baby Jesus, shepherds, angels, animals]*
Oh, no! I forgot someone! In fact, I forgot three people! Please help me look for the three wise men. I must have lost them around here. *[Encourage the children to look around the front of the church for the wise men.]*
There they are! I'm so glad you found them. Christmas just wouldn't be Christmas without the three wise men. What can you tell me about these people? Why are they important to us? What gifts did they bring to the baby Jesus? Let's read the story of the wise men in the Bible. *[Read Matthew 2:1–12.]*
You know, I'm not the only one who keeps forgetting the wise men and their gifts. Most people in our country have forgotten all about the wise men and their special day called Epiphany. Say that word with me, "Epiphany." On Epiphany, we remember how the wise men followed that bright star in the East over a long and dangerous road until they found Jesus in Bethlehem. Then they honored him as King over all nations by giving *Jesus* their gifts, not each other like we do

on Christmas.

Let's celebrate Epiphany this year by giving our gifts to Jesus, just as the wise men did. Those who have gifts are invited to come forward and tell us about your gifts.

**Prayer:** Dear Lord, please accept these gifts in honor of the birth of Jesus. Amen.

# And Jesus Was Baptized

**Purpose:** To demonstrate the three forms of baptism: by sprinkling, immersion, and pouring. To lift up what is common to all Christian baptisms.
**Scripture:** Mark 1:9–11.
**Materials:** Baptistry or font. May want to use a baby doll for demonstrating. Have water in baptistry or font if convenient.

**Sermon:** Children, let's meet this morning by the baptistry (or baptismal font).

*[After the children have gathered]* We don't use this baptistry every Sunday, so I wonder what it is used for. What do we do with this water?

A baptistry is for baptizing people. Jesus was baptized by John the Baptist. Jesus tells us to be baptized so that the world will know that we are his followers. Let's read the story in the Bible about Jesus' baptism. *[Read Mark 1:9–11.]*

Almost all Christians baptize, but we don't all do it in the same way. Let me show you three ways to be baptized. Watch me carefully and see if you can find out what is the same about all of the baptisms.

One way Christians baptize is by sprinkling a baby, and sometimes a teenager or an adult. How many people in our church were baptized by sprinkling? When a pastor baptizes by sprinkling, she or he takes the baby and sprinkles a few drops of water on the head and says, "I baptize you in the name of the Father, the Son, and the Holy Spirit." *[Demonstrate with a baby doll.]*

A second way Christians baptize is by immersion, usually of a teenager or an adult. How many people in our church were baptized by immersion? May I have a volunteer to show how baptism by immersion is done? I'll do a "dry" baptism on you. I won't put you under the water. When a pastor baptizes by immersion, he or she goes into a large baptistry, or sometimes a river or creek, until the water is up to the waist. Then

27

the pastor invites the person to be baptized to come into the water. The pastor says, "I baptize you in the name of the Father, the Son, and the Holy Spirit." Then the pastor gently lowers the person into the water until he or she is all wet. Then the pastor lifts the person out of the water again. *[Lower the child backwards and lift him or her to a standing position.]*

A third way a Christian can be baptized is by pouring. Has anyone in our church been baptized by pouring? When a person, a baby or an adult, is baptized by pouring, the pastor takes a cup of water and pours it over the head of the person and says, "I baptize you in the name of the Father, the Son, and the Holy Spirit." *[Demonstrate with a doll and water from the baptistry or font, or demonstrate with a child without water.]*

So, there are three ways to be baptized as a Christian. In our church, we baptize by _____. Did you see or hear anything alike in the three kinds of baptism— by sprinkling, immersion, and pouring? All use water, right? And all use the words, "I baptize you in the name of the Father, the Son, and the Holy Spirit," the three names for God.

**Prayer:** Dear God, you ask us to be baptized. Please teach us what baptism means, and help us to accept the baptisms of other Christians. Amen.

*Epiphany #3*

# Tempting Chocolate Ice Cream

**Purpose:** To explain the word "temptation." To assure that everyone is tempted.
**Scripture:** Luke 4:1–14.
**Materials:** A lunch box and an ice cream cup.

**Sermon:** Do you know what kind of box this is? *[Show them a lunch box.]*

How many of you take a lunch box to school?

I want to tell you a story about a little girl who was tempted to do something wrong with her lunch box.

The little girl's name was Lynn, and she was in the first grade. Lynn loved ice cream, especially chocolate ice cream. How many of you love chocolate ice cream?

Well, one day Lynn went through the lunch line at school and saw a cup of ice cream. It had vanilla ice cream on one side and chocolate ice cream on the other. Lynn wanted the ice cream so badly she could taste it. So, when no one was looking, she snatched a cup, threw it in her lunch box, and quickly closed the lid before anyone saw her. *[Demonstrate with the ice cream cup and the lunch box.]* Then, when she reached the woman at the cash register, she only paid for her milk.

Now, Lynn knew that what she did was wrong. But the next day when she went through the lunch line, there was that ice cream again, that chocolate ice cream, and she hid it in her lunch box as she did the day before. Lynn stole ice cream every day in the lunch line for several weeks until one day the woman at the cash register caught her.

Why was it so hard for Lynn to stop stealing the ice cream? She knew that stealing was wrong, so why did she do it? Lynn was being tempted by the ice cream. When you are tempted by something, you really want it, even though you know that it is wrong for you and a bad thing to do. Everyone, no matter how young or how old, is tempted by things that are bad for him or her.

Jesus was tempted, too. He was tempted three times by things that he really wanted. *[Read selected portions from Luke 4:1-14.]*

Unlike Lynn, Jesus did not give in to his temptation and take what was bad for him. He remembered what God had told him, and that gave him the strength to do the right thing.

**Prayer:** Dear God, sometimes we really want things that are bad for us. Please remind us to ask you for help whenever we are tempted. Amen.

# Being a Part of a Team

**Purpose:** To imagine the disciples and the church today as a team.

**Scripture:** Luke 6:12–16.

**Materials:** Pieces of equipment from various team sports: e.g. a baseball mitt, a kickball, a basketball, a football helmet, a hockey stick.

**Sermon:** What is your favorite sport? What sports or games do you like to play with your friends? Do you watch sports on TV? *[Give the children time to share.]*

I have some equipment from different team sports. Which sport uses a bat? a helmet? a ball like this? *[Let the children identify each team sport.]* Although these sports use different balls and equipment, they have something in common. They all need a team in order to be played.

How many of you have played kickball? *[Allow the children time to respond.]* In kickball, you need more than one player on each side. You need a team. You need someone to roll the ball, someone else to stand on first base, someone else to stand on second base, another person to stand on third base, and at least one more person to play catcher near home plate. In kickball, then, you need a team of five players. In baseball you need a team of nine players. In football you need a team of eleven players. And in basketball, you need a team of five players.

Jesus needed a team, too. Even though he was the Son of God, he could not spread the good news of God's love all by himself. He needed help. So, one evening as the sun was setting, he left behind all of the people who were following him from town to town and took a long walk into the hills. He went there to be alone and to talk to God in prayer. He thought about all of his followers and asked God to help him choose from among them the very best people to be on his team. After he had stayed up all night in prayer, he walked out of the hills

31

and asked twelve people to be on his team. Do you remember what we call the twelve friends of Jesus? We call them "disciples."

Now this team of disciples did not sit back on the sidelines and let Jesus do all the work. They jumped right in and helped Jesus teach, preach, and heal the people. They were a big help to Jesus, and each of the twelve disciples was a part of his team.

Today, *we* are Jesus' disciples. We are part of his team to spread God's love to everyone. Our team is called the church. Some people think that all of the work of the church is done by the minister. But the minister's job is to be a coach. Do you know someone who is a coach at school or Little League? What does the coach do? Does the coach play the game while the team sits on the sidelines and watches? Of course not! The coach's job is to help each player work with the others and all the players to work together as a team.

A minister's job, then, is like a coach's job. The minister helps members of the church work together as a team to tell the world about God. A minister cannot do all the work alone. A minister does not even conduct a worship service alone. A minister does not clean up the sanctuary, print the bulletins, pass out the bulletins at the door, welcome visitors, prepare the communion trays, pray, preach, sing, play the organ, serve communion, and collect the offering all alone! She or he relies on the janitor, the secretary, the ushers, the deacons, the elders, the worship committee, the organist, the choir director, and the choir to help with all the work of conducting a worship service. Every worship service is a team effort.

How thankful I am that we have so many wonderful people on our team at church to share all of the work! God has called each one of us to be on this team we call *[your church's name]*. Our minister *[name or names]* is the coach now, but our owner will always be the Lord.

**Prayer:** O God, we want to be on your team, just like your disciples. Help us to work together to tell the world about your love. Amen.

# Doing What the Bible Says

**Purpose:** To demonstrate that in order to understand the Bible, one must do what it says.
**Scripture:** Matthew 7:24–27.
**Materials:** A Bible. A sign that reads, "Go out into the congregation and shake someone's hand."

**Sermon:** Do you know what this book is? *[Show the children the Bible.]*

That's right, this is the Bible. Can anyone tell me why the Bible is so important? *[Listen to their answers.]*

Those are some good answers. The Bible is special because we believe that God helped people to write the Bible. We call the Bible "God's Word." / Well, the Bible needs to be read in a very special way if we are going to understand it.

Who can read this sign I made? *[Let several children read it.]*

Now, I want someone to really read it. *[Let someone else read.]* You all have the words right, but I want someone to really read the sign. Look very carefully this time. What does it say to do? *[Let another child read it.]*

Now, read it as you are supposed to read the Bible. Read it, and then go do it. *[Have a child read the sign, and then get up and do what it says.]*

God can't speak to us through the Bible unless we are willing to *do* what we *read.* There are two parts to reading the Bible: (1) read and (2) do.

Jesus says: If you read these words of mine in the Bible, think about how you can use them in your life, and run out to act on them before you forget what I've taught you. But if you read the words, slam the Bible shut, run off and do whatever you like, and ignore what I've taught you, then you are a foolish person.

So, there are two steps to reading the Bible.

What is Step One? Read the words.

What is Step Two? Do what the words say.

33

**Prayer:** O Lord, we are just learning how to read books. Remind us when we read your book, the Bible, that we need to read the words and do them. Amen.

# The Bible, a Treasure Map

**Purpose:** To imagine the Bible as a treasure map.
**Scripture:** Matthew 6:19–21.
**Materials:** Four envelopes labeled: Clue #1, Clue #2, Clue #3, and Clue #4. A card inside each envelope. On Clue #1, "Read Galatians 6:14." On Clue #2, "Read Matthew 28:19." On Clue #3, "Read Psalm 40:9." On Clue #4, "Read Psalm 119:103." Tape Clue #2 to a cross in the sanctuary. Tape Clue #3 to the baptistry. Tape Clue #4 to a pew or chair in the congregation. Clue #1 stays with you. Have with you a Bible with the above passages bookmarked for easy reading. In a large Bible in the sanctuary, hide one stick of sugarless gum for each child expected.

**Sermon:** What do you think when you hear the words "hidden treasures"? Do you think of a pirate with a black patch over one eye? When I hear the words "hidden treasure," I think of a story Jesus told about a man who was walking through a field listening to the birds and the wind blowing through the trees when suddenly—"Ouch!"—he stubs his big toe on a strange-looking chest. When he opens the chest, he sees money and jewels—too much to count. He looks around to see if anyone is watching him. When he is sure he is alone, he hides the chest under a bush and covers it with branches. Then he runs home and sells his car, his TV, his VCR, his stereo, his computer, even his house, so that he has enough money to buy the field. He sells all he has to buy that hidden treasure.

Jesus says the love of God is like that man's hidden treasure. He said, "Where your treasure is, there will your heart be also." If we knew what a treasure God's love is, we would give up everything, even sell everything, to have it.

How do we find God's treasure? One way is through the Bible. The Bible is like a treasure map. Let me show you.

Here is Clue #1. Who will read it for us? It says, "Read Galatians 6:14." Let's look up that scripture and read it aloud: "Far be it from me to glory except in the cross of our Lord Jesus Christ." Where is the cross in our sanctuary? Look to see if Clue #2 is there.

Now let someone else read Clue #2. It says, "Read Matthew 28:19." Let's look up that scripture and read it for everyone to hear: "Go therefore and make disciples of all nations, baptizing them in the name of the Father and of the Son and of the Holy Spirit." Where do we baptize people? Look for Clue #3 near the baptistry.

Will you read Clue #3? It says, "Read Psalm 40:9." Please read for us this verse of scripture: "I have told the glad news of deliverance in the great congregation." Where is the great congregation? Someone go out into the great congregation and see if you can find another clue.

Our last clue is #4. It says, "Read Psalm 119:103." Where does the scripture say to look next on our treasure hunt? "How sweet are thy words to my taste, sweeter than honey to my mouth!" Where do we find God's written word in the sanctuary? In the Bible. Go and see if there is a treasure in the pulpit Bible.

*[After the children have found the sticks of gum]* God's words are sweet to us, like this gum. They are a treasure, and the Bible is a treasure map.

**Prayer:** God, you are our treasure. Help us to find you with our treasure map, the Bible. Amen.

# Don't Be a Pinhead

**Purpose:** To remind the children that mean teasing and insults can hurt someone deeply.

**Scripture:** Matthew 7:1-5.

**Materials:** With a magic marker, draw a face and hair on an inflated balloon. Be careful; it smears easily. You will also need a hat pin or large pin.

**Sermon:** I have a friend I'd like you to meet. Her name is Geraldine. Geraldine is a pretty happy person. She likes to play the piano and ride her bike with her friends. But every once in awhile she has some trouble with some people in her school who are called the "pinheads." *[Show the children the pin.]*

You see, pinhead people are the kind of people who like to pick on others. They like to tease in mean ways and make little hurtful comments like:

"Geraldine's dumb," or "Geraldine is a fatso," or "Geraldine is ugly."

*[As each insult is stated, pretend to jab the pin at the balloon. The children will anticipate the balloon exploding, so have a long list of insults. On the last insult, pop the balloon, and wait for the children's reaction.]*

You know, Geraldine is like you and me. We can take just so much teasing, insults, or picking on from the pinheads of the world. Jesus says: Judge not, so that others won't judge you. In other words, don't pick on each other. Don't insult other people, even if everyone else is doing it at school, at home, or even at church. Don't be a pinhead.

**Prayer:** Dear God, help us not to pick on other people: on our little brother, our older sister, or someone at school. We don't really want to be mean old pinheads. Amen.

# Accepting People
## (Martin Luther King, Jr. Sunday)

**Purpose:** To show that labels, especially when applied to people, can be misleading. To relate Jesus' parable of the good Samaritan to the work of Martin Luther King, Jr.

**Scripture:** Luke 10:25–37.

**Materials:** One can of fruit or vegetables. One can of cat food, with a label over it from a same-size can of tuna. One can opener.

**Sermon:** *[Hold up can of fruit or vegetables.]* Can you tell me what is in this can?

How did you know what was in the can? You read the label.

Now, can you tell me what is in this can? *[Hold up the can of cat food.]* Are you sure it is tuna fish? Read the label carefully. I'd love a tuna fish sandwich for lunch, so I'll just open this can. *[Start using a can opener to open the can.]* I'll mix it with some mayonnaise and put it on my favorite bread. Wait a minute! This doesn't look or smell like tuna fish. What do you think it is? *[Take off the tuna fish label.]* It's cat food!

In Jesus' parable of the good Samaritan, he tells us to be careful about labels. Some people had labeled Samaritans as bad people. That's why Jesus told this story about a good Samaritan who helped the man who had been beaten and robbed. Martin Luther King, Jr. also taught us to be careful about labels. In his day, which was not very long ago, black people were labeled as bad people, and white people were labeled as mean people. That's why Martin traveled around the country to try to get rid of those labels once and for all. Martin told us not to label people as good or bad, nice or mean, smart or dumb. Martin had a dream that one day people would not be judged or labeled because of the color of their skin but by the content of their character—by what is inside them. That's the same thing Jesus taught with the story of the good Samaritan. *[Read Luke 10: 25–37.]*

**Prayer:** Dear God, please stop us whenever we start labeling people as bad, mean, or stupid, just because of the color of their skin or the way they look. Remind us to always look inside of persons to find out who they really are. Amen.

# Christians Only

**Purpose:** To introduce the names of different denominations. To show that Christians can and need to work together, regardless of denomination. To lift up the Week of Prayer for Christian Unity.

**Scripture:** Galatians 3:28.

**Materials:** Church listings in the yellow pages, telephone directory, or newspaper. Diamond-shaped yellow sign with the words "Christians Working Together."

**Sermon:** The other day I was looking to see if our church's name was in the newspaper (or yellow pages), and I was surprised to see how many churches there are in our area. There are ___ Episcopal churches, ___Catholic churches, ___Baptist churches, ___Disciples of Christ churches, and ___churches of our own denomination, which is _____. There are so many churches and so many different denominations!

I wonder how many people in our congregation grew up in a different denomination than this one. Raise your hand if you grew up Methodist. Lutheran. Church of Christ. Presbyterian. Etc. Any other churches? Please speak up.

I think it's great that all of us can work together, even though we come from different churches. We're doing here in our church what needs to happen all over the world— Christians working together regardless of denomination.

I've made a sign to remind us of what the Week of Prayer for Christian Unity is all about (or that the Bible teaches us that we are one in Christ Jesus). It is like those road signs you see that warn us to watch out for people fixing the road. Those highway signs read, "Men Working." My Christian Unity sign reads, "Christians Working Together." Notice that I didn't write, "(your denomination) Working Together," or "Presbyterians Working Together," or "Methodists Working Together."

All Christians need to work together because, as the Apostle Paul wrote, "We are all one [or the same] in Christ Jesus our Lord."

**Prayer:** O God, help us to follow your teachings so that all Christians can work together for you. Amen.

# Introduction to Lent

## Dixie Holt Deen

Lent begins with Ash Wednesday and is the prelude to the church's great observance of Easter. Just as the adult congregation needs preparation and guidance through this season, so do the children. The season includes forty weekdays plus the six Sundays just prior to Easter. Forty is a symbolic number used in many biblical references. For those churches using liturgical colors, violet is the color of Lent.

This period of time is one of deep introspection for the total church. It is traditionally set aside for personal reflection and repentance through study and prayer. Heavy emphasis is placed on the teachings of Jesus, particularly forgiveness, confession of sin, personal relationship with God, prayer, and love. These are areas to which both adults and children can relate. It is important to choose words carefully in talking with children about this season. Lent is the season through which children can grow into a better understanding of the meaning of Easter.

# Prayer

**Purpose:** To emphasize the importance of prayer for Christians.
**Scripture:** Matthew 6:9–13.
**Materials:** None.

**Sermon:** Good morning! How are you doing today? Did everyone sleep well last night?

Let's think about when we were preparing to go to bed last night. What do you like to do before you climb into bed? *[The children will answer things like: take a bath, put on pajamas, brush their teeth, get a drink, kiss their parents good night, and say their prayers. If the last is not mentioned, you can say that you always say your prayers before going to sleep.]*

What do you do when you say your prayers? *[This will probably elicit responses such as: kneeling with parents at the side of the bed or saying prayers after getting into bed.]*

What is prayer? *[Accept answers as the children give them, and repeat them in the children's vocabulary. Emphasize that whenever we talk to God, it is special and important. It is our personal time with God.]*

What do you talk to God about? *[Allow time for children's responses.]*

I often talk over a problem with God, thank God for something, ask God for help or guidance, or maybe share a bit of good news with God.

Besides bedtime prayers, are there other times when you might like to talk to God? *[Some possibilities might be the blessing before meals, in church worship, when we are happy, or when we are sad, or when we are scared.]*

I usually close my eyes when I pray and sometimes fold my hands. *[Demonstrate, and allow them to fold their hands before more discussion.]*

Some people kneel down in order to pray. Some pray in song. Many of our hymns are written as prayers, and the music was added later. You may know of another way of offering your prayer to God. *[Give the children the opportunity to respond.]*

Jesus prayed to God too. Did your realize that Jesus spent much time in prayer? Jesus spent much time teaching about God, but he also allowed himself time to share with God the thoughts, plans, hopes, and problems that he had. He wanted us to talk to God, too, and he taught us a prayer that we could use. This prayer is called the Lord's Prayer. Some of you might already know all the words. Before you get too much older, I am sure you will know it from memory. Christians all over the world know the Lord's Prayer. Every Sunday many Christians say the Lord's Prayer as a part of their morning worship service. We have other opportunities to pray within the service, but this is special because we can do this together. How many of you know the Lord's Prayer?

I like to share a prayer here each Sunday with you children as we close our time together. I think today it would be special if we could say the Lord's Prayer together. If you are not sure of the words, that's okay. Say the ones you know. *[You may wish to invite the rest of the congregation to join this moment if it is appropriate to the service. If you choose not to end with the Lord's Prayer, the prayer below could be used to culminate the thought.]*

**Prayer:** Dear God, we like being able to talk with you. Thank you for being there. In Jesus' name. Amen.

## Saying "I'm Sorry"

**Purpose:** To help the children gain a better understanding of what it means to do wrong and how to say "I'm sorry."
**Scripture:** Luke 19:2–9.
**Materials:** Broken pencil. Bible.

**Sermon:** Good morning, boys and girls. I hope you are all having a good day.

I want to tell you a story about a woman who started out the day with a difficult morning. She was late in getting up and had to hurry to get to church on time. She left home so quickly she forgot her pen so she borrowed a pencil from the secretary's desk when she arrived. Since the secretary was not there on Sunday, she wasn't able to ask permission to borrow the pencil. It was a good pencil, and she used it to write some important notes. Then she misplaced the pencil. Later she found it, but it had been stepped on and broken. *[Hold up pencil so the children can see.]* When the church opened the next day and the secretary would check her desk, her pencil wouldn't be there. The woman who took the pencil felt sad and didn't know what she should do next. If she didn't mention it, maybe the secretary wouldn't know who borrowed it. But the woman would know, and she would still feel sad.

What would you do? *[Follow the discussion of the children, and affirm their answers. Some will be right on target, and others might not have thought through their answers. Listen and follow up.]*

You have all given some good advice. I think the only way the woman will feel better is to tell the secretary how sorry she is and ask her forgiveness for borrowing the pencil without permission. I think it would also be a good idea if she offered to replace the broken pencil with a new one.

Do you think the secretary will forgive the woman? Would you forgive her if it had been your pencil? *[Allow for discussion.]*

In the Bible there is a story about a man who was well known for the wrong things that he did. He was a tax collector and became very rich because of the way he collected taxes. He had heard about Jesus coming to the town where he lived and wanted very much to see him. By the time this man reached the roadway, there was already a large crowd. Being a very short man, he couldn't just stand at the back of the crowd and still see Jesus coming down the road. *[Ask the children if they understand how the man felt behind all those tall people.]*

The next idea the man had was to climb a tree and look down upon the road. So the short man found a tree and climbed onto a low branch. He felt he had a good view and would be able to see Jesus. Well, Jesus came along the road and saw the man sitting in the tree. Some of you have guessed who this man was. What did Jesus say to him? You can say it with me: "Zacchaeus, make haste and come down; for I must stay at your house today." Is that the way you remembered it? *[Some children's versions are much simpler, but with your Bible in hand you can read directly from the story in Luke.]*

Zacchaeus quickly climbed down and was very excited to be taking Jesus to his own home. Others in the crowd who knew that Zacchaeus had done many wrong things could not understand why someone as important as Jesus would want to be a guest in his home.

Zacchaeus decided that he needed to share some of his great wealth, so he promised Jesus that he would give half of everything he had to the poor. He also said that if he had cheated anyone, he would give them what he owed them four times over. *[Hold up four fingers to emphasize.]* Jesus was pleased with Zacchaeus' decision. It was a good way to say, "I'm sorry."

**Prayer:** Dear God, sometimes we do things that maybe we should not. When we are wrong, help us to say we are sorry. In Jesus' name. Amen.

# Forgiveness

**Purpose:** To stress the importance of forgiveness.
**Scripture:** Matthew 18:23–35.
**Materials:** Bible.

**Sermon:** Good morning, girls and boys. How are you this morning?

Let's see if any of you can tell me about being angry. Yes, we can make our faces show our anger. *[Make a cloudy face yourself.]* And the tone of our voice is hard and sometimes loud. *[Change the inflection of your voice.]* When I am angry, I find I cannot do a good job in my work nor can I enjoy playing. How about you? *[Allow the children to respond about ways their anger affects them.]*

Your discussion suggests that we do not really like to be angry. Jesus teaches us how to get rid of our anger. Does anyone have any ideas about what he said?

Yes, he wants us to love everyone. Can you love someone who does something wrong toward you? In order to love someone after you have been angry with him or her, you must practice forgiveness, according to Jesus.

Can you all say that word—forgiveness? Is this a word you recognize? What is forgiveness? *[Give the children a chance to give their definitions.]* Forgiveness means forgetting the wrong thing that someone has done toward you and letting the anger go away from you.

How would you tell someone that you forgive him or her? *[Wait for answers.]*

You could simply use the words, "I forgive you," couldn't you? Sometimes a hug is a warm way of telling someone you forgive her or him. There are other ways, too.

What happens to our faces when we are no longer angry with someone? *[Show a softer face.]* We can smile again. I feel much better inside, too, when I am not angry. I can work or play with the person I was angry with and be friends with that person again.

47

One of the stories Jesus told about forgiveness was about a king who called before him a servant who owed him a large amount of money. The servant had no way of paying such a large amount, so the king ordered him to be sold along with his wife and children, plus all of their possessions, in order to pay the debt. The servant fell to his knees and begged the king not to do this. He said, "Lord, have patience with me and I will pay you everything." The king felt sorry for the servant, so he released him and forgave him the debt.

But this same servant saw a fellow-servant who owed him some money, which was not much compared to the large amount he himself had owed to the king. The first servant insisted that the money owed him be paid immediately. When the fellow servant begged, "Have patience with me and I will pay you everything," the first servant had the fellow servant put into prison until the debt was paid.

When other servants saw what had taken place, they went to the king to report what had happened. The king was as upset as they were. He called the first servant before him. The king was angry. He said, "You wicked servant! I forgave you all that debt because you asked me, and should you not have forgiven your fellow servant as I have forgiven you?" [Ask the children what they think.]

Sometimes we get angry with ourselves when we make a mistake or do something we should not. It is important to forgive others. It is also important to forgive yourself and give yourself the opportunity to try again. Do you know how to forgive yourself? I often need God's help with this, and I talk to God about it in prayer.

**Prayer:** Dear God, we are learning about forgiveness. Help us to remember to forgive when we are angry with other people or with ourselves. In Jesus' name. Amen.

# You Are Important!

**Purpose:** To emphasize that each of us is important to God.
**Scripture:** Matthew 18:12–14.
**Materials:** Picture of a lamb or sheep. Bible.

**Sermon:** It is so good to be here this morning! I like being here with you in our church. How about you? *[Give the children an opportunity to respond.]*
Tell me about God. What do we know or feel about God? *[Affirm all answers in as positive a way as you can. The children will have various responses. Your acceptance of their honest thoughts is important. Some interpretation on your part may guide the discussion toward the individual's relationship to God.]*
I have many of the same thoughts and feelings about God. I am me because God made me. You are you because God made you. You are my friends and we are all a part of this church because we all believe in God. *[Hold up your picture of a lamb or sheep, and ask the children what is in your picture. As you tell the story, point to your picture whenever you mention sheep.]*
There is a story Jesus told about a man who had a hundred sheep. Each day the man took his sheep across the mountains to the fields to eat the grasses. And each evening he would travel back across the mountains with the sheep. As he would put them in their pen each night, he would count them to be sure they were all there. He would count to one hundred before he would lock the pen. One evening as he was putting the sheep in their pen, he counted ninety-seven, ninety-eight, ninety-nine; and there was no one hundred.
Even though he was very tired, the man went back to the fields to look for his one lost sheep. Sheep are not like some other animals that can find their way home. When the man finally found his lost sheep he was overjoyed, for each one of his sheep was important to him. He would have searched for

any one of them that was lost.

God loves each of us and cares for us like the man who cared for his lost sheep. When we are lost, God is there for us. We can talk to God through prayer and know that God will listen. We know that God is present in our lives. Can we think of some ways God is present? *[Some possible answers may be: the existence of our church, our health, new babies, good friends, or whatever is pertinent for your group.]*

Just as we are certain that lost sheep was glad to rejoin the other sheep in the pen, we are thankful that God has blessed each of us in so many ways. God has been generous with us by giving us many gifts. For instance, to be able to sing is a gift that we can use to sing praises to God and to add beauty to our worship. Your church school teacher is using a gift to teach in preparing a lesson and sharing it with you each Sunday as you study about Jesus' teaching and about God's world. The person who keeps our building clean and in good repair is also sharing a gift from God. What are some of your ideas about ways we can use God's gifts to us? *[Repeat the children's answers, and include some of the gifts or talents of which you are aware among the children and among adults all of the children know.]*

From what we have discussed this morning, I would say that each of us is very important to God.

**Prayer:** Dear God, we are thankful that each of us is important to you. Thank you for loving us. In Jesus' name. Amen.

# A Symbol of Love

**Purpose:** To gain a deeper understanding of love.
**Scripture:** Mark 12:30–31.
**Materials:** A big red heart cut from paper. You could have a number of smaller hearts to share with the children.

**Sermon:** Good morning, girls and boys. I am so happy to be here with you again this morning.

Today I have with me a symbol to share with you. Does anyone know what a symbol is? If I were talking to a group of musicians and did not spell the word symbol, one might think I was talking about the musical cymbals that you strike together to make a loud noise. But in the church we have many symbols. A symbol is a picture that immediately lets us know what it means. Here is my symbol. *[Hold up the red heart.]* It sounds like you all know that a red heart means love.

Let's talk about love. Can you touch it? Can you hold it? Is it squishy or solid? How would we describe love to someone who does not know what love is? *[Children will have a variety of responses. Older children will probably give situational descriptions. Younger ones will be able to identify what or who they love.]*

From what you are telling me, I think love has a lot to do with feeling. Since I cannot hold it in my hand, maybe I can hold it in my heart. *[Hold up the red heart.]* I think it is a warm, good feeling. What do you think? *[Allow for their interpretation.]*

When is love around? Do you think it is in the sanctuary right now? I wonder if you carried any in as you arrived this morning. Did you smile when you first saw your teacher or a friend? Were you a helper in your class? How did you see love this morning? *[Use more personalized questions of your unique situation if children are slow in responding.]*

Love is such a wonderful word. Jesus used it often. When asked what he would say was the greatest of all the commandments in the world, he said, "You shall love the Lord your God with all your heart, and with all your soul, and with all your mind, and with all your strength." The second commandment Jesus gave us was, "You shall love your neighbor as yourself." Have you heard that part of the Bible before? It sounds like Jesus felt love was very important.

We know that God loves us, and Jesus tells us to love God. Because God loves me, I feel good and want to share that love with others. I love you, and to remind you that I love you I have a symbol for you. *[Give each one a similar heart.]* As you look at this heart, I hope it will remind you of the love we shared with each other this morning and that it continues even when we are apart.

*[Another possibility would be to share hugs within the group. As the children return to their pews, they might like to share a hug with members of the congregation along the way. Suggest this before the closing prayer. Some might not feel comfortable doing that, so leave it open for each child to decide. Another way to involve the congregation would be to give each child several hearts and ask the children to distribute them.]*

**Prayer:** Dear God, we do love you as Jesus taught. We thank you for the love in your world. In Jesus' name. Amen.

## Hosanna in the Highest
### (Palm Sunday)

**Purpose:** To celebrate Jesus' entry into Jerusalem.
**Scripture:** Mark 11:1–10.
**Materials:** A real palm branch or one cut from construction paper. One for each child would be ideal.

**Sermon:** Good morning, girls and boys! What a glorious day! Today is Palm Sunday, and we are all celebrating. *[Wave the palm branch. If you have enough, pass out the palm branches to the children. Tell them each of them needs a palm branch to help you tell the story.]*
This was an important day in Jesus' life. He was going to Jerusalem with his disciples. Many of his followers knew he was coming too and were excited that Jesus was coming to their city. They had heard he was going to be riding on a small animal, like a young donkey colt.
Jesus had sent two of his disciples ahead to get an animal for him to ride on. They found a donkey colt just where Jesus said it would be. Then they started their journey into Jerusalem. The people were standing along the roadway waiting. The roads in those days were not paved like ours today. They were smooth dirt, and when you walked on them your feet and sandals got dusty. The air was also heavy with dust, especially when so many people were gathered together to stir it up.
In order to protect Jesus from all the dust, the happy followers had spread their own coats on the dusty path. They also broke off large branches from trees as they prepared for Jesus' coming. By waving them *[Wave the palm branches]*, they kept a nice breeze flowing for their king, Jesus. Some also lay their branches on the dusty road for him to pass over.
Many also sang as Jesus passed, "Hosanna to to Son of David! Hosanna in the highest!" Has anyone ever heard the word "hosanna"? When do you think we use it? It is a very

53

happy word, used to express much joy and usually spoken with a loud voice.

This was an occasion when "hosanna" was just the word to use to tell Jesus how happy these people were to see him.

Would you please help this morning as we are worshiping on this special occasion? Let us stand and face the congregation and repeat our words of celebration with a loud and happy voice. *[Remind them to wave their palm branches if they have them.]* "Hosanna to the Son of David! Hosanna in the highest!"

Now let everyone in the congregation join us: "Hosanna to the Son of David! Hosanna in the highest!"

*[Depending on your church's plan for Holy Week and the age of your children, this would be a good time to prepare the children for the events that will be happening through the coming week. You can tell them it was important for Jesus to be in Jerusalem because of the events of the week. Maundy Thursday and Good Friday will have been observed before you talk with the children again. It is important to mention these days on Palm Sunday as a part of the season of Lent. Easter Sunday is sometimes too full of activities and thankful praise for any reflection on the preceding week. Churches approach Maundy Thursday and Good Friday in a variety of ways, so follow the custom of your church, and consider the children as you choose your words. Use simple and honest language and be sincere. What children learn about this aspect of the Christian faith is the foundation on which they will build all of their lives.]*

**Prayer**: Dear God, we are very happy to celebrate Jesus' journey to Jerusalem. Amen.

# Introduction to Easter

## Sue Amyx

Easter is the most important celebration in the life of the church. Even though many people have attached a secular meaning to Easter, it is the responsibility of the church to make Jesus the focal point. We are helping children celebrate that Jesus lives!

Easter is a difficult season for children to understand. The church has just come through Palm Sunday, the Last Supper, and the crucifixion. And now we are trying to say to children, who think in concrete terms, that Jesus, who was crucified and died, is now alive. Resurrection, for Jesus, meant that death was not the end. God raised Jesus to new life. Jesus lives, and that is something to celebrate.

It is important that the children experience, at their level, the joy and excitement in the life of the church at Easter. The significant point of Easter is that Jesus lives and that we experience joy because he lives. We celebrate the good news throughout the church. To be included in the celebration gives children a sense of belonging and importance in the church family. They hear and learn the story; they share in the spirit of joy and celebration; and we are giving them a solid foundation on which they can build their faith.

One word of caution as you talk about new life and tie it to Easter. Do not overemphasize that Easter is a time of happiness because things are new in the spring (i.e. new leaves, grass, and flowers). This is important as you talk about new life, but it is not the significance of Easter. Remember, the significant point of Easter is that Jesus lives and that there is great joy and celebration because of the good news.

# Christ Has Risen Indeed!
## (Easter Sunday)

**Purpose:** To help the children realize that Easter is a joyous time and a time to celebrate because Jesus lives.

**Scripture:** Mark 16:1–8.

**Materials:** Decorated eggs made out of construction paper.

**Sermon:** Today is a special day in the life of the church. What is the holiday we celebrate today? *[Easter.]* That's right. I want to share a very special story with you this morning. The story is found in the New Testament and goes like this:

Jesus had died on Friday. His sad friends lovingly took his body from the cross and put it in a tomb. The tomb was like a cave. The entrance to the tomb was closed with a huge rock to keep out animals and robbers. That night and all day Saturday Jesus' mother and his friends tried to comfort each other. They were so sad! Early on Sunday morning some of the women went to the tomb. "Who will roll away the stone from the tomb so we can put the spices there that we brought for Jesus' body?" they wondered.

When they got to the tomb, they couldn't believe what they saw. The stone had been moved! They rushed inside the tomb, but Jesus' body was not there. They could not understand how the tomb could be empty. They knew Jesus' body had been taken from the cross and put in the tomb. They knew that Jesus had died.

Suddenly an angel spoke to them. "Don't be afraid. I know that you are looking for Jesus of Nazareth. I have good news for you. Jesus is not dead. He is alive! Go now and tell his disciples the good news. Jesus will meet them in Galilee."

The women were happier than they had ever been as they hurried off to tell the others, "Jesus lives!"[1]

The women were so excited, and there was so much to celebrate because Jesus lives!

I have something I want to share with you this morning. Eggs have become a popular symbol of Easter. What do you think about when you see eggs at Easter time? *[Allow time for comments like candy, egg hunts, new life, baby chicks.]*

All that is true, but what I want us to think about this morning is that eggs can remind us of new life. You see, God raised Jesus to new life, and that is good news and exciting.

To share the good news that Jesus lives, in some countries of eastern Europe, Christians greet their friends with "Christ is risen!" The friend replies, "Christ has risen indeed!" As a part of that greeting, they might also give their friend a brightly decorated egg with a cross, butterfly, or flower, all symbols of Easter, on it.

What I have for each one of you are two decorated eggs *[not candy, but made out of construction paper]*. I would like for you to greet your friends, teachers, or family with the special greeting and then share one of your decorated eggs. If you do this at home and you have eggs from your Easter egg hunt, you might use one of those eggs. Do you remember what the greeting was? Let me help you. Let's do it together. The first person says, "Christ is risen!" And the friend responds, "Christ has risen indeed!" Good.

Now, before I greet you and give out the eggs, let's have our prayer.

**Prayer**: Dear God, thank you for your Son, Jesus. We thank you that Jesus lives. That is good news and it makes us happy. Help us to share that good news with others. Amen.

*[If there are a lot of children, have someone close to the front help you hand out the eggs. It will save time. Greet the children with "Christ is risen!" After they respond, ask them to take one of their eggs to someone in the congregation. The children are to use the same greeting when giving out the eggs.]*

# God Is Always There

**Purpose:** To help the children realize that God is always with us and helps us.
**Scripture:** Exodus 15:22—16:36.
**Materials:** None.

**Sermon:** There are many stories in the Bible about God being with and helping God's people. One is the story of Noah. Another is the story of Moses. God was with Esther and helped her and her people. There are lots of similar examples in the New Testament of the Bible. The story I want to share with you this morning is in the Old Testament of the Bible. It is about God being with and helping the people of Israel.

After the people had crossed the Red Sea, they camped out for a while but they ran out of water. So they moved on until they came to a pond called Marah. The water there was very bitter, and the people could not drink it. They got angry at Moses because of the taste of the water. Moses talked to God, and God showed Moses a special kind of log to throw into the water to make the water taste good. The people really liked that.

They continued on their journey and soon they began to run out of food. Again they were very unhappy and angry. Moses talked to God, and God told Moses, "I will send bread down from heaven like rain. Every day the people will gather enough to eat for that day. Now, on the sixth day, they will need to pick up enough food for the seventh day, because everyone is to rest." God sent the manna, and the people gathered it and made it into loaves or cooked it like cereal.

They were happy for awhile, but they wanted more. They claimed they were getting weak because all they had was bread. So God told Moses, "Each morning you will have manna to eat, and the evening you will eat meat." That evening God sent a flock of birds, called quails, to nest in the desert. The people caught them and roasted them and had meat to eat. Moses told the people, "Now God has fed you and taken care of you."

Was God with the people of Israel? *[Yes.]* How did God help them? *[Give the children time to answer. If you have older children, you might ask how God is helping us today.]*

This is only one story and example in the Bible about how God is with us and helps us. Just as God was with the people of Israel and helped them, God is with us today and helps us.

**Prayer:** God, you are always there, and we are glad. Thank you for always being with us. Thank you, God, for the ways you helped people long ago and for the ways you help us today. Amen.

# God Forgives

**Purpose:** To help the children see that God forgives us and gives us the ability to forgive others.
**Scripture:** Luke 15:11–32.
**Materials:** This story could be told easily using a flannel board.

**Sermon:** This morning I would like for us to talk about forgiveness. What does the word "forgive" mean to you? *[Allow time for their responses.]*

Jesus told a story, concerning forgiveness, about a father and two sons. You will find the story in the Bible, in the New Testament, in the book of Luke. It goes something like this.

There once was a rich man who had two sons. The younger son decided he wanted his share of what the father owned right then. The father gave it to him. The young man took all of his things and went to a far country.

While he was gone, he spent all of his money having fun. When his money was gone, he didn't have any food or a job. Do you know what kind of job he got? He got a job feeding pigs. He got so hungry he thought the food the pigs were eating looked good!

Suddenly he thought to himself, "Why am I doing this? My father's servants have more than I have right now. Why should I stay here and die of hunger? What I am going to do is go back to my father and admit that I have sinned against God and done wrong to my father. I'll admit that I'm not good enough to be his son and ask to be one of his servants."

So the young man started home to his father's house. Before he got to the house, his father saw him and came running out and greeted him. The son did just what he said he would do and admitted that he had been wrong. Do you know what the father did? *[Allow time for responses, and continue the story.]*

The father listened to the son and all that he had done

wrong. And then he did an amazing thing. He called to the servants to bring the best clothes to be put on his son and gave him a ring and shoes. The father was so excited to have his son home that he had a party celebrating his son's return.

The older son came in from working in the fields and heard the music and asked what was going on. A servant told him that his younger brother had returned and that his father was having a party.

How did the older brother respond? Did he rush in and greet his brother? No, the older brother was angry, and he wouldn't go in to the party. His father came out and begged him to come in, but the older brother replied, "Look, all these years I've worked hard for you and you never gave me a party. But when this son of yours shows up after wasting so much money, you kill the fatted calf and have this huge party!" His father said, "Son, you are always with me, and everything I own is yours. But we have reason to celebrate because your brother, who we thought was dead, has returned home!"

Who in this story was forgiven? Who forgave him? [Allow time for the children to respond.]

The older brother was having a little trouble forgiving his brother. He was pretty angry. We may find it hard to forgive someone sometimes when they hurt us or do something wrong. Sometimes we want to get even, or we just stay mad.

The father is a good example of forgiveness. In fact, God is like this father. The father accepted the son's statement that he had done something wrong and then went on to celebrate his son's return. God accepts our "I'm sorry" and goes on. By talking to God about it and asking for God's help, we can forgive others, even when it is hard to do. God gives us the ability and the courage to do that.

**Prayer:** God, we all make mistakes and hurt others sometimes. Thank you for forgiving us. God, help us, especially when it is hard, to forgive others. We pray in Jesus' name. Amen.

# The Greatest Kind of Love

**Purpose:** To help children see how, in Jesus, God set an example of loving for us.
**Scripture:** John 15:9–17.
**Materials:** None.

**Sermon:** Love is a word that is familiar to all of us. We hear the word a lot, but I'm not always sure that we know what it means. I have an example of love that I want to share with you this morning. Sometimes when we look at an example of how to do something, it helps to discover what it is. And it certainly helps us to see how we can love.

I want to share with you today a scripture from the Bible about love. It is something that Jesus told his disciples a long time ago. I am reading today from the Good News Bible, Today's English Version. I am reading from the New Testament, in the Gospel of John. "I love you just as my Father loves me; remain in my love. If you obey my commands, you will remain in my love, just as I have obeyed my Father's commands and remain in [God's] love. . . . My commandment is this: love one another, just as I love you. The greatest love a person can have for [one's] friends is to give [one's] life for them. And you are my friends if you do what I command you. . . . This, then, is what I command you: love one another" (John 15:9, 10, 12–14, 17, TEV).

God tells us that we are to love everyone and that God's love is for everyone. That is part of what Jesus was talking about when he said, "Love one another, just as I have loved you." This is how Jesus lived his life.

How did Jesus show his love for his friends? *[Allow time for children to respond with things like: He made them well, he forgave them, he ate with sinners, he died for them, he talked to people other people wouldn't talk to, he helped people who were different from him, etc.]*

These are good answers. That is how Jesus showed his

love. Now, how can we show love for our friends? *[Allow time for children to respond with comments like: help them, share toys with them, not fight, include other kids that might not be included in a game, send cards to people who are sick, etc. The children should have some good responses here, but you may have to clarify; if they say "help them," ask how they can help.]*

One thing you might want to remember is that there are lots of people we can help through giving money that we could not help in any other way. We have special offerings in our church that help people with special needs. Many times the people we help with these special offerings are much different from us. They do not have enough food. They may not have a place to live or enough clothes to wear. Some children may need help learning how to read. When you give money to these offerings, that is one way you are sharing love.

Another thing Jesus said was that "The greatest love a person can have for [one's] friends is to give [one's] life for them." Jesus gave his life for us. He loved us that much. We are Jesus' special friends. He loved us a lot to give his life for us. We probably will never have to give our life like Jesus did, but we are called to love others in lots of different ways. We have talked about some of these ways this morning.

Let's read part of the scripture one more time: "My commandment is this: love one another, just as I love you. The greatest love a person can have for [one's] friends is to give [one's] life for them. . . . This, then, is what I command you: love one another."

**Prayer:** Thank you, God, for loving us so much that you gave us your Son. Jesus set an example for us in how he loved his friends. Help us to share our love with others. Amen.

*Easter #5*

# A Caring Family
## (Family Week or Mother's Day)

**Purpose:** To help the children explore ways that their parents love and care for them.
**Scripture:** Luke 2:41–51.
**Materials:** None.

**Sermon:** Families are very important. Today we are celebrating Mother's Day, and mothers certainly are very special. I would like for us, however, to talk about our entire family, ways we show love, and ways we care for each other.

I have a story from the Bible that I want to share with you. It is found in the New Testament and is about Jesus when he was about twelve years old.

Every year Jesus and his parents went to Jerusalem for the Passover festival. When Jesus was twelve they made their normal trip to Jerusalem. When the festival was over, Mary and Joseph started back home, thinking Jesus was with friends in the group.

After traveling an entire day, they started hunting for Jesus and discovered he was not with the group. They looked and looked for him. They went back to Jerusalem and looked all over for Jesus. Mary and Joseph were really worried because they could not find Jesus.

They looked for Jesus for three days. Finally, on the third day they found him in the temple sitting with the Jewish teachers, listening to them and asking all kinds of questions. The people in the temple were surprised at how intelligent Jesus was and how well he answered questions. His parents were surprised and relieved when they found him in the temple.

Jesus' mother said to him, "Son, why have you done this to us? Your father and I have been terribly worried trying to find you." Jesus answered his mother, "Why did you have to look for me? Didn't you know that I had to be in my Father's

64

house." His parents really didn't understand his answer.

Anyway, Jesus went back to Nazareth with his parents and was obedient to them, which means he minded them. He did what they said.

Have you ever been lost? [Allow time for response.]

It can be a scary time for you, but think about your parents. Jesus was not lost. He knew exactly where he was, but he was separated from his parents, who were very worried about him. They loved him and wanted him to be safe and not hurt. Probably his mom and dad were relieved and angry all at the same time.

How did Jesus' parents show that they cared for him? [Allow time for their response.]

How did Jesus show that he cared for his parents? [He went home and obeyed them.]

How do your families show that they care for you? [Allow time for answers such as: take care of them, provide food, clothing, and a house for them to live in, etc.]

How can you show your parents that you care and love them? [Allow time for answers like pick up toys, mind parents, share things, say thank you, etc.]

You know, I think Jesus was a pretty normal boy. We don't have much information about him as a boy, but I think he was probably in trouble on occasion. But I think he also set a good example for us when, in our story today, we discover one of the ways he showed that he cared for and loved his parents—he obeyed them. I think that is an important lesson for us to learn.

**Prayer:** God, thank you for our families and all the ways that we care for each other and share our love. Help all of us to care for each member of our family. Amen.

# Praising God with Music

**Purpose:** To help the children realize that there are many ways to praise God and one way is through our music in worship.
**Scripture:** Psalm 147:1.
**Materials:** None.

**Sermon:** David praised God through his music. Miriam took a tambourine in her hand and praised God with song and dance when the Hebrew people were safe after crossing the Red Sea.

We can praise God, too, through our music. Tell me about the music in our worship. When is there music in our worship? *[Allow time for children to respond with things like the prelude, hymns, during communion, choir singing, etc.]*

Is the music in our worship all the same? Is some of it fast, some slow, some loud, some soft? *[Allow children to respond about what they think the music is like.]*

The music is not all the same, and that is okay. In fact, that is good.

Let's take time to think about the hymns we sing in our worship. A hymn is a song that is a gift to God. Hymns can be fast or slow. They can be stories, scripture, prayers, or even a word repeated several times. By singing hymns in our worship, we are praising God. One hymn that we use that children like to sing is "All Things Bright and Beautiful." It is a good children's hymn, and it is a song praising God and celebrating God's creation. It is a happy song.

Another hymn children like to sing is "Kum Ba Ya." Does that hymn move as fast and sound as happy as "All Things Bright and Beautiful"? *[No.]* It may not be as fast, but the music is nice and it has special words. We are asking God to "Come by here" in our worship and in our lives. That's what "Kum Ba Ya" means. That is another way of praising God.

There are times when there is music but we are not singing. When are some of those times? *[Allow time for the children to respond—prelude, communion music, offertory, postlude.]*

The organ music during prayer time often is quiet and slow. The organ music during the offering many times is louder and faster than the music during communion. Both are fine ways in which we can praise God.

We can praise God with our music, whether it is with our voices or with instruments like the organ or piano. Now that we have talked about music in our worship on Sunday mornings, I hope you will notice the different kinds of music and listen to it, remembering it is a way of praising God.

**Prayer:** God, thank you for the many ways that we can praise you. Today we thank you especially for the gift of music. It is good to be able to sing praises to you. We pray in Jesus' name. Amen.

# What's Special About Where We Worship?

**Purpose:** To help the children be aware of the art in their sanctuary and to thank God for the gifts and talents people shared through the art because of their love of God.

**Scripture:** 1 Kings 5—8.

**Materials:** Articles in the sanctuary: stained glass windows, pictures, crosses, candles, etc.

**Sermon:** This morning I would like for us to talk about the place where we worship on Sunday mornings. I want to share a story from the Bible. It is in the Old Testament and is about a beautiful temple built by King Solomon and the people of Israel. Some of you may know about King Solomon and the temple because of what you have studied in church school.

Solomon remembered that God had said to his father, King David, "Your son will build my temple in Jerusalem." Solomon began work on the temple. Hundreds of cedar and pine trees were floated in rafts on the Mediterranean Sea to Solomon. He sent men into the mountains to cut stone.

The temple was beautiful. There were carvings of angels, palm trees, and flowers on the walls. All the floors were laid with gold. Everything on the altar was made of gold. Even the hinges for the doors were gold. It took thousands of workers more than seven years to build the temple.

The place where the people worshiped in the days of King Solomon was called a temple. Today we call it a sanctuary. We are worshiping today in a sanctuary. Our sanctuary doesn't have gold or lots of wood carvings, but it has many pretty things that add to our worship experience.

Look around the sanctuary and tell me what kinds of art, pictures, or symbols you see. *[Let children respond: stained glass windows, candles on communion table, etc.—whatever is appropriate in your sanctuary.]*

Our sanctuary was not built the same way Solomon had the temple built. We don't have the gold, bronze, or wood carving. But the things you pointed out have special meaning for us in our place of worship today. Special people gave of their time and talent to do the paintings. The stained glass windows help tell us more about God and Jesus. The crosses are symbols that remind us of Jesus. *[Cite specific things in your sanctuary.]*

Could we still worship here if we didn't have all these things? Sure we could. The place would be very plain. Having these beautiful windows, pictures, and symbols helps us to remember that people gave special gifts and talents to our church because they wanted to share their love for God in this way. These items also help us to focus our thoughts on God, and they remind us of Jesus and his life as we worship together.

At the end of the story of Solomon, when the people finished the temple, they sang and thanked God for the temple. Their hearts were filled with joy because of the goodness God had shown to Solomon and all the people of Israel.

Let us take time to thank God for our beautiful place to worship, our sanctuary, and for the talents and gifts people have shared because of their love for God.

**Prayer:** God, thank you for this beautiful place to worship. Thank you for the people who built it and for their talents and gifts that have been given to the church. Thank you for the symbols, pictures, and stained glass windows that help to remind us of you. Amen.

------

[1]From Living the Word, Level 4, Spring, 1988, p. 40. Copyright American Baptist Board of Christian Education. Used by permission.

# Introduction to Pentecost

## John T. Hinant

The first half of the church year is a time to experience the life of our Lord. The second half, which we call the season of Pentecost, is a time to live out in community the meaning, message, and ministry of Jesus. It is the longest season in the church year, beginning with Pentecost Sunday, when we are reminded that Christ's presence is to be experienced by his followers in a new way, as the Holy Spirit.

Children can understand the fact that the church had a beginning and that we celebrate its birthday on Pentecost Sunday. They can appreciate the fact that something wonderful and exciting happened, which we call the gift of the Holy Spirit. This gift gave the people then and now the power to do things together that they could not have done alone or without God's help.

The season of Pentecost is a time in which we celebrate our life together as a church—a church in which people of all ages, from the youngest to the oldest, are important. Green is the color of this season, reminding us that it is a time to experience together spiritual growth and ongoing life. It is a time when all of us, including children, can be empowered by the Holy Spirit to carry the ministry of Jesus into the world.

To help leaders plan for this lengthy season, four subsections are included: the church, discipleship, creation, and special days. Emphases found in many congregations during this time of the year are the focus of these sermons.

70

## Let's Have a Celebration
### (Pentecost Sunday)

**Purpose:** To help children know how and for what purpose the church was born.
**Scripture:** Acts 2:1–4a.
**Materials:** Sparklers, if available.

**Sermon:** What is the most exciting day you ever had? Was it your birthday? Was it Christmas? Was it the day your baby brother or sister came to live with you? Or was it the day you got your new bicycle? *[Let the children respond.]*

The church had an exciting day that we enjoy remembering. It is called "Pentecost." That's a hard word that means fifty, and the day is called Pentecost because something very exciting happened fifty days after Easter. The church began. So today is like a birthday party, isn't it? It makes us happy to know that we have the church and we can be a part of it.

Jesus' friends had gone to Jerusalem. They were lonely and frightened just like you when someone you love has to go away. They weren't sure what to do and, if they'd known what they were supposed to do, I'm not sure they could have done it. But they got together and prayed for God's help.

All at once something exciting happened. It was so wonderful that they could only describe it as the sound of a strong wind. If you had been there, you might have described it as the sound of a jet engine on an airplane passing nearby. Whatever it was, it was so loud they couldn't hear anything else. They stopped praying and just listened, wondering what else might happen. And they saw something that looked like fire, and each one of them felt it. It must have been like the Fourth of July, except the fireworks came very close and didn't burn. When I hear this story, I think of sparklers. *[A sparkler may be burned at this point to help awaken the children's excitement about what had happened.]*

But that wasn't all that happened. People had gathered

71

in Jerusalem from all over the world. They spoke many languages and couldn't understand one another. It was as though each one of you spoke only one language and each of them different. If Becca spoke only English, and Matthew spoke only Spanish, and Crystal spoke only Russian, and Scott spoke only French, and each of the rest of you spoke another language, and all tried to speak, no one would understand anything anyone else was trying to say and it would just sound like a lot of noise.

But something very strange happened. It didn't matter what language someone else was speaking, each person heard it in his own language. Becca could hear Matthew speaking Spanish, but she would hear it in her own language, English. Crystal would speak Russian, but Scott would hear the language he could understand, French.

Wasn't that strange? But God wanted them to hear and understand what was being said because God had something special to tell them through one of Jesus' special friends, Peter. Peter hadn't always been brave. Sometimes he had disappointed Jesus. But today, Peter stood up tall and straight and told the people all about Jesus. He could do this because he didn't feel alone or weak. He felt that Jesus was with him in a special way, and it made him feel better. He had that special feeling we sometimes call the Holy Spirit.

Peter told the people that they had treated Jesus badly, but if they were sorry God would forgive them. They could feel just like Peter because God would give them the special feeling Peter had.

A lot of people did believe what Peter told them—about three thousand. They became friends of Jesus' followers and learned from them what Jesus taught and what Jesus did. They shared what they had with the poor and prayed together and worshiped God together and ate together with glad and generous hearts. And that was the beginning of the church of which you and I are a part.

**Prayer:** Thank you, God, for the church. Help us to have that feeling Peter had so we can love Jesus and help the church do the kind and wonderful things Jesus did. Amen.

# A. The Church

## *John T. Hinant*

"Who is a member of the church?" We too easily answer, "Those who have made their confession of faith in Jesus Christ and have been baptized." This definition of membership severs children from the body of Christ of whom they are a part. Children may or may not be baptized, but they are still important and valued members of this community of faith that we call the church. The contribution they can make to all of us and the ministries we perform is a valuable one.

The strength of the church is found in its life together as a worshiping community. Just as the disciples were "all together in one place," it is important that all of us who are part of that community, including the children, experience together the corporate worship of the church. The church that practices hospitality toward its children during its most important hour together is the church that will reap a harvest of grace and strength.

The participation of children in worship, not as performers but as persons sharing their gifts as they receive ours, is to be treasured, not in some sentimental fashion but as authentic expressions of faith. These expressions can strengthen the faith of all of us as we experience and share the love of God and the power of the Holy Spirit.

# How Big Is Your Family?

**Purpose:** To help children understand that the church is a family of which they are an important part.
**Scripture:** Ephesians 2:19.
**Materials:** None.

**Sermon:** Let's talk about our families today. Some of us live in big families, and some of us live in small families. Some of us live with our mothers or fathers, and some of us live with both. Some of us have brothers and sisters, and some of us are the only child. Some of us have grandmothers or grandfathers living with us, and some don't. Some have pets that are part of the family, and some don't. We have different kinds of families, But each one of us has a family—the people with whom we live who love and care for us. Tell us about your family. *[Take a few moments to let the children share something about their families.]*

Living in a family is good, isn't it? Wouldn't we feel sad and lonely if we didn't have a family? Our Bible tells us that God sets the lonely in families (cf. Psalm 68:6). Being a member of a family is part of God's plan. Most of the time the people in our families make us feel good and happy because they take care of us and tell us how much they like us and need us. And they don't just talk about it; they do it. They take care of us and give us good things to eat and clothes to wear. They give us presents on our birthdays and at Christmas and sometimes just to surprise us. They take us to playgrounds and the zoo and see that we get to school on time. Can you think of some of the the things your family does for you? *[Allow a few moments for some of the children to share the good things their families do for them.]*

But your families need you, too. I'm sure that the people who love you and take care of you would say, "I don't know what I would do without Billy or Shelly or Janet." *[Name some of the children in the group.]*

Your family needs you just as much as you need them

because you're you. Just as there are ways in which they show their love for you, there are ways in which you show your love for them. Can you tell us some of the ways you show your love for your family? *[Allow a few moments for some of the children to share the ways in which they show their love for their families.]*

We've been talking about those with whom you live, but there are others who are also a part of your family. There are grandmothers and grandfathers and aunts and uncles and cousins and special friends. All of us have those special people who are like family, with whom we get together to share good times and sad times, people whom we love very much and who love us. The more we think about it, the larger our family becomes.

The church is also our family, and in it we are to love one another and to care for one another just as we do with the family with whom we live. Each one of us is an important part of the church family. Isn't it exciting to know that the church needs you? None of us needs to feel that we don't belong, for we are all part of the church. Paul, one of God's special heroes, says that because God loves each one of us we are no longer strangers, but we are members of the family of God.

The family of God is the church. Yes, you are part of that family. You belong in church, where all of us are like brothers and sisters. Some of us are like big brothers and big sisters, who are to make a place for you and care for you in this wonderful family God has given us that we call "the church."

God wants this special family to show the world how much God loves us and how loving we can be. We are to make room for the stranger and the visitor within our special family until there is no one who doesn't share the kind of love we know in our families. When this happens, everyone will feel like brothers and sisters, with Jesus as a kind and helping big brother and God as a parent who will always love us.

**Prayer:** Thank you, God, for our families, who make us glad. Thank you for everyone who loves and cares for us. We are glad for the church and happy that we are a part of this family in which we can know and share your love. Amen.

## Building Bridges and Washing Dishes

**Purpose:** To help children understand that to be a Christian is to be a servant.
**Scripture:** John 13:15.
**Materials:** A chisel and a hammer, a broom and a scouring pad, a bucket and a towel.

**Sermon:** I used to think that to be a good Christian all you needed was a Bible and maybe a hymnal, but I'm finding out that it takes all kinds of tools if you want to follow Jesus.

I've brought just a few of the tools that some people in the church have found to be useful. Take this chisel and hammer, for instance. What in the world do they have to do with being a Christian? Well, at least one person thought they had a lot to do with it.

Benezet lived in France 800 years ago. He was a boy who took care of his mother's sheep in the hills along the Rhone River. It was a dangerous river, and it must have worried Benezet to see people trying to cross it in small boats, which were often swept away or overturned by the swift current. Many of them were drowned. Benezet must have wondered why there was no bridge. But bridges were expensive and hard to build. The more Benezet watched what was happening, the more certain he was that God wanted him to build a bridge that no one else would build.

One day he rushed into church shouting, "God wants me to build a bridge." Can you imagine what people thought when this boy interrupted the church service to tell them that God wanted him to build a bridge? The minister said that if God wanted a bridge, the people in the church would help.

Benezet gathered a group of workers who were called "Brothers of the Bridge." They raised money and built the bridge. It took ten years to build, using hammers and chisels to cut and shape the stone. When it was finished it was a beautiful bridge that still crosses the Rhone River near Avignon. But most important, it enabled the people to cross

76

the river safely. The Brothers of the Bridge built bridges everywhere. Benezet was a good servant because he did something that needed to be done, and because of him travel became easier and safer for everyone.

Brother Lawrence was another one of God's servants. He was a big, clumsy man who had been crippled in battle. There wasn't much he could do to be of help in the monastery where he lived. No one thought he could do much, so they put him in the kitchen, where he swept and scrubbed pots and pans for thirty-one years. Brother Lawrence was very happy in the kitchen. If this was the way he could be of help to others, then this was what he wanted to do. It was difficult for him to sit still and pray, just like it's difficult for some of you. He felt closer to God when he was busy washing dishes and cleaning up the kitchen. He learned to pray while he was working. Other Christians came to his kitchen to learn how to pray. Soon Brother Lawrence, with his happy smile and cheerful voice, was helping everyone in his church feel closer to God. Brother Lawrence learned that he could be closer to God while serving others with his broom and scouring pad.

Jesus thought it was very important for us to learn to be servants. He was a servant himself. This bothered his friends because they thought that it was better to have other people doing things for them than to be doing things for other people. Jesus wanted them to know how important it is to be a servant. One time he tied a towel around his waist and took a basin of water and washed his friends' feet. This embarrassed them because they thought he was too important to do this for them. But he said, "I have given you an example of what you should do for one another" (cf. John 13:15).

Benezet and Brother Lawrence knew what Jesus meant. They discovered that in the Christian community we call the church, one of the most important things we can learn is to be a servant—a person who does something for someone else that needs to be done, whether it is building a bridge, washing dishes, opening the door, kissing a hurt, or helping to carry a heavy load.

**Prayer:** Thank you, God, for servants. Help us to be servants, too. Amen.

# Everyone Has Something Special to Share

**Purpose:** To help children know that each one of them has a special gift to share with the church and that the church needs and wants their gifts.
**Scripture:** John 6:5–14.
**Materials:** None.

**Sermon:** God created each one of us different. No one looks like anyone else, and I'm glad, aren't you? If we all looked alike, Cindy Lou would look just like Patrick, and Patrick would look just like Jeremy. *[Use names of children in the group.]*

Wouldn't it be dull and boring? Why, we'd have to wear name tags so people would know who we are because each one of us would look just like everyone else. Even your mothers and fathers would have to check your name tag to be sure they had the right boy or girl. If you wanted to know what I look like, all you'd have to do is look in the mirror because you'd look just like me. Wouldn't that be awful?

But we're all different and I'm glad. God made each one of us different, and that makes us special. Not only do we look different but we are different in other ways, too. Some of us sing well. Some of us draw pretty pictures. Some of us can even stand on our heads. What is something you do well? *[Allow a few minutes for the children to share something they do well.]*

God has given each one of us a special gift, something we do well. It might be a happy smile. Do you know that your smile can travel around the world? Yes, it can. If you smile at someone here in church who is sad and lonely, he'll begin to smile.

Later he may take your smile to someone who is grumpy and out of sorts, and that grump can't help but smile. That person may smile at someone who is hurting, and for a little while the pain is forgotten. Your smile begins to get around, and before long it may travel around the world. See how important the gift of your smile can be?

You have lots of gifts to share. There is a story in the Bible that reminds us that boys and girls have important gifts we all need. One time Jesus was being followed by a crowd of people. They had followed him all day because he was healing people, and they wanted to see him and hear what he had to say. They followed him to a hillside, where he sat down. The people came closer, and Jesus saw that they were hungry because they hadn't eaten all day. Jesus asked one of his friends if they had enough bread to feed the people, but his friend Philip said that it would take far more money than they had.

Andrew, another one of Jesus' friends, said, "There is a boy here who has a few fish and some bread. He's willing to share it, but I don't think it's enough to feed very many people." Jesus had all the people sit down on the grass, and then he took the boy's five loaves of bread and two fish and thanked God for them. Then he passed them out among the five thousand people. And do you know what happened? There was enough for everyone! When the people saw that the little boy was willing to share what he had, they began to share what they had and there was enough for everyone to eat. Peter, another one of Jesus' friends, must have remembered the little boy who was willing to share when he wrote in a letter: "As each has received a gift, employ it for another, as good stewards of God's varied grace" (cf. 1 Peter 4:10).

No gift, if given in love, is unappreciated by God. Once long ago there lived a minstrel, a young man who could turn handsprings and backflips, who could walk on his hands and balance a ball on his feet, who could juggle five plates at a time. He was talented and made much money. But more than anything else, he wanted to serve the church. So he gave up everything he had and went to live in the church.

But all he knew how to do was to leap and to jump, to turn somersaults and to dance. Everyone else would recite prayers and sing songs, so he felt very sad. But late at night he would slip into the church, and there he would do for God what he did best. God was very pleased with his gift, and the tumbler was happy. The minister was curious, so one night he slipped into the church to watch the tumbler. He was surprised but not angry. He wanted everyone to watch because the tumbler's gift was a beautiful gift that no one else could offer.

**Prayer:** Thank you, God, for giving us gifts to share. Help us to share our gifts whatever they are. Amen.

# Everywhere We Go

**Purpose:** To help children know that the church is a worldwide community with a world mission to serve people.
**Scripture:** Matthew 28:19–20.
**Materials:** A flying carpet and lots of imagination.

**Sermon:** The last thing that Jesus asked his friends to do while he lived on earth with them was this: "Go and tell everyone in every country about me so they will want to follow me and be part of my church. Show them how to do all the things I have taught you to do for one another, and I will be with you forever."

This morning we're going to take a trip to see how well Jesus' followers have done what he asked. I hope you ate a good breakfast because it's going to be a long trip. My friend, Aladdin, loaned me his flying carpet for the trip. The reason you can't see it is because it's magic—it's in your imagination.

Now if you will step to either side, I'll unroll it. There it is. Isn't it pretty? It's very old; that's why there are worn spots.

Now if you will all get on it we're almost ready to go. We don't have seat belts; you'll have to hold hands so no one falls off. Ready? Okay, we're ready to take off. Let me check with the control tower first. Control Tower, this is Flying Carpet. Number One requesting permission to take off. Over and out. Flying Carpet Number One, this is Control Tower. Use the center aisle to the door, and then fly very high so you can't be seen. We don't want anyone to think you're a flying saucer. Over and out.

Are you ready? I'm going to count down and take off. Are you ready? Three, two, one. Here we go! Whew! It takes your breath away, doesn't it? Take a deep breath, and we'll start looking for churches and Christians doing what Jesus told them to do.

We won't have time to see everything, but we'll take a quick trip around the world to see what's happening. Let's go south first. See that island? It's Haiti. The people are very

81

poor there. There are some people right there beside that shelter without any walls. They're Christians, too. Some of them are learning how to sew on machines our own church helped provide. When they learn how to sew, they can make clothing and sell it for money to help feed their families.

Lean to the right while we bank toward Latin America. See those mothers with their babies? They're standing in line so Christian nurses can give the babies shots so they won't get sick. And over there is a school that teaches children how to read and write. Christians made that possible. And look, see all that mud! It slid down a mountain and covered some of the houses. Christians are helping them move the mud and rebuild the houses.

Let's travel west now. Here we are over Thailand. Christians gave that farmer a water buffalo to plow his fields so he could raise rice for his family to eat. And that pretty building is a school where young Thai men and women are learning to be ministers and to tell the people about Jesus, just like Jesus wants us to do.

I wish I could spend more time in India, but if you'll look quickly as we fly over, you'll see people at a well dug by Christians. Now the people can have clean water to drink and to water their fields so they can grow food to eat. And there's a hospital that takes care of sick people with cataracts so they won't be blind. Christians are busy in India, aren't they?

We'll fly over Africa now. See those people in the desert beside that truck? They look skinny, don't they? They must be very hungry. They're getting milk for their babies and food. The truck has a sign on it that says, "Church World Service." That's what the church is doing there. And here in Zaire is a big church and a lot of people being baptized. Christians there are busy telling people about Jesus, and people are becoming Jesus' followers.

Everywhere we go, all around the world, Christians are busy telling people about Jesus and helping people because that is what Jesus wants us to do.

**Prayer:** Thank you, God, for Christian friends around the world who show people how much you love them. Amen.

## The More We Get Together

**Purpose:** To help children know that everyone who believes that Jesus is Lord is a Christian and part of the church, even though they go to different churches and worship God in different ways.
**Scripture:** John 17:20–21.
**Materials:** Imaginary magic eyeglasses.

**Sermon:** How many of you boys and girls live in a house or an apartment? I believe that's all of you. Do you have your own room, or do you share a room with a brother or sister? Tell us about it. *[Allow a few moments for the children to respond.]*

We all live somewhere, and we all have a room that is ours, even if we share it, where we sleep and keep our clothes and toys and special things that belong to us. But that doesn't mean we don't like our families or our friends who live in other rooms in other houses, does it? And it doesn't mean we're different from our brothers and sisters and good friends.

The church is something like a house with many rooms, in which God's children live most of the time in their own rooms but join together at special times to worship and to do God's work. The church building is one room in God's house in which we live, but there are many other rooms, with many other people who believe in Jesus and try to live like him.

Let's see if we can look in some other rooms that we call churches in God's house. My friend, Aladdin, needed his flying carpet this week, but I found enough magic eyeglasses for all of us. Here, each of you take one. Put them on. Now turn the knob just over your right ear, and we can stay right here and see churches just down the street and around the world.

There are a lot of churches, aren't there? They don't all look like ours, do they? There's a big one with a tall tower made out of stone with beautiful stained glass windows. And over there is a small white wooden church with a steeple. See that one with a roof made out of grass? It's just a hut. There's a brick church and one made out of dried mud painted pink. There are all kinds of church buildings, aren't there?

I guess it doesn't matter what kind of building the people meet in, does it? What matters is what the people are doing. If you'll push the button on the end of the earpiece just behind your left ear, we can see and hear what's going on inside these churches. Ready? There are some people singing a hymn. I don't recognize the words, but I recognize the tune. It's "Joyful, Joyful, We Adore Thee." Look over here. These people are praying. It sounds like Russian. In that big church on the right is someone in a robe telling the people about Jesus. They're taking an offering over in the little church. You know what? The people wear different kinds of clothes, they meet in all kinds of churches, they speak different languages, and they do things differently. But they're all worshiping God.

Remember your own room at home? Even though you have your own room, you get together with the rest of the members of your family to eat. Some meals are special, like Thanksgiving or Christmas or your birthday dinner. In the church we get together to have a special meal called communion. And that's something we all do because Jesus prayed that we might share a meal and remember him. And even when we can't meet in the same place, we know that we are sharing the same meal and are together in what we're trying to do. Christians around the world share this meal because we are brothers and sisters in God's house. When I think about this, I feel like singing a song. Will you sing too?

The more we get together, together, together,
The more we get together, the happier we'll be.
For your friends are my friends, and my friends are your
friends.
The more we get together, the happier we'll be.

**Prayer:** Thank you, God, for churches in which people share your love and sing your praises. Help us to remember that we are your children who share the same home with Jesus, who wants us to get together as brothers and sisters. Amen.

# Peanut Butter Friends

**Purpose:** To help children know that there are things they can do to make friends with people around the world.
**Scripture:** 2 Corinthians 5:18.
**Materials:** A jar of peanut butter.

**Sermon:** Do you recognize what I've got in my hand? Yes, it's a jar of peanut butter. Do all of you like peanut butter? There aren't many boys and girls who don't. I brought it because I want to tell you a story about a jar of peanut butter and the friends it helped to make.

Betty Jane and her mother had gone to the grocery store to buy the groceries for their family. Betty Jane liked to shop with her mother because she got to pick out her favorite cereal, and sometimes her mother let her pick out a special treat. But today Betty Jane wasn't thinking about cereal or treats. She was trying to decide what to take to her church school class for the food pantry. Her teacher had told her that the food pantry helped the church feed hungry people. But what should she buy? And then she remembered that the best gift is something you like yourself. She knew exactly what to buy. She went right past the jelly counter to the peanut butter and picked out the biggest jar she could find, and that was what she took to church for the food pantry.

Several weeks later she had almost forgotten the peanut butter. Reverend Butler told her about a family that came by their church for help. The father had lost his job in another city because the factory where he worked had closed. He and his wife loaded their two children, Wilma and her baby brother, and everything they could carry into their old station wagon and set off to find work in another town. They had been living in their station wagon for almost a week and were almost out of money when they came to Betty Jane's town and to her church to get help. Reverend Butler gave them food, including Betty Jane's peanut butter, and helped the father find a job and a place to live.

Reverend Butler introduced Betty Jane to Wilma and asked her to help Wilma get started in school. Betty Jane was excited. They would be in the same class. But Wilma was worried. Would the boys and girls like her? Would they think her clothes funny? Would they think she talked weird?

The next morning Betty Jane's mother took Betty Jane to pick up Wilma for her first day at the new school. Can you remember your first day in a new school? It can be kind of scary, can't it? But Betty Jane knew just what to do. She told the other boys and girls, "This is my new friend, Wilma." Wilma felt good knowing that she had such a good friend who would help her get acquainted and not let people laugh at her. It wasn't long before Wilma was a part of the group.

One Sunday their minister, Reverend Butler, announced that the church had agreed to resettle a refugee family. Betty Jane and Wilma didn't know what this meant, but Reverend Butler explained it. He said there were people who had nowhere to live because wars, or earthquakes, or floods, or other terrible things had destroyed their homes. People with no place to live were called refugees, and God wanted their church to do its part in finding homes for these people.

He said the church was going to make a home for Siyoum, a boy who lived with his older sister and her husband in a tent in a refugee camp in Ethiopia, waiting for a home. His father had been killed, and his mother had died of starvation.

Later, Reverend Butler showed Betty Jane and Wilma a picture of Siyoum and told them that Siyoum would need friends like them when he and his family arrived. Betty Jane and Wilma thought he looked awfully skinny, but their minister told them it was because he didn't get enough to eat.

Betty Jane and Wilma were excited. Siyoum would arrive next week, and everyone was helping to get an apartment ready for the family. The children had been asked to bring food. Betty Jane and Wilma knew what they would bring. Can you guess? Yes, peanut butter. And that is how Betty Jane and Wilma and Siyoum became peanut butter friends.

**Prayer:** Thank you, God, for old friends and new friends. Help us to treat our friends well so we don't lose them. Amen.

# B. Discipleship

## Jim Benton

Because the season of Pentecost (or ordinary time) is the longest season of the church year, there are many opportunities for exploring the "ordinary" business of being a Christian people. In this section of sermons on discipleship, scriptures have been chosen from a variety of texts from the New Common Lectionary for the season. They not only provide fourteen children's sermons about discipleship but also fourteen models for adapting biblical material into the language of children.

Almost all of the sermons are stories retold in the language of children. Repetition and liveliness (even silliness) are two components of that language, and the preacher must grow comfortable with those tools. But, more than that, the preacher must learn to explore these stories that Jesus was told, stories that were told about Jesus, and stories like the ones Jesus told, with a sense of discovery and eagerness— not as if explaining them but as if discovering them, not so much teaching the children but inviting them to enter a different world, the fascinating world of Jesus and his friends.

Worship is an event that invites all to enter a different world, and the sense of discovery and imagining that the preacher of these sermons can convey is the same sense that we should all bring to worship. Discipleship as explored here is not so much prescriptive (help others, make peace, choose wisely) as descriptive of a way of belonging in a community called "Jesus and his friends," or "the community at worship," or "the church."

# Toys, Toys, and More Toys!

**Purpose:** To share with the children the fun and the danger of acquiring things. To raise the question of what priority we give to the things that we have.
**Scripture:** Luke 12:16–21.
**Materials:** None.

**Sermon:** *[Hints for telling the story: It will be helpful to insert the names of some of the latest children's toys and fads as part of the acquisitions of the children in the story. Choose names of children in your congregation, or let the children choose names for the characters.]*

Once upon a time there was a very rich man. He bought his children lots of toys and clothes and candy and ice cream and computer games and videos and stereos and everything you can imagine. At first, his children were very happy to eat ice cream all day and watch television and play with one toy after another after another after another after another.

But one day the toys and games and candy wrappers were piled up so high that the daughter (whose name was Lisa, I believe) said, "I don't even have a place to lie down!" And she started looking everywhere in her room for her bed. She looked behind the VCR and under the stereo. She looked underneath the pile of dolls and behind the bookcase. Finally, underneath a huge pile of stuffed animals she found—her brother Brian!

"Lisa! Lisa! You found me at last! I thought I was going to be trapped in here forever! Do you know the way to my room?"

"I was looking for my bed," she said. "I don't know where anything is anymore."

"Let's go talk to Mother and Daddy about this," said her little brother, "if we can find the way to the door."

They crawled over piles of clothes and through a jungle of board games and dirty clothes and finally found the door. Then they went looking for their father and mother. But they were working late. It seemed like they just worked all the time. Lisa and Brian decided to wait for them to come home instead of taking a chance of getting lost again in their rooms.

When their mother and daddy came home, Lisa said, "Daddy, I can't even find my bed anymore! There are too many toys and things in my room."

And Brian said, "Mother, I got lost in Lisa's room this morning, and she didn't find me until this afternoon. There are just too many toys and things in my room."

"This is what we'll do," their daddy smiled. "We'll pull down your rooms and build larger rooms, and there we will store more and more toys. Then you lucky children can say, "Lucky us! We have every toy in the whole world!"

And their mother said, "And you can take your ease and eat all the candy and drink all the colas and watch all the television you want to. You'll never have to say that there are too many toys in your rooms again!"

But before their mother could call the builder to get started, before their daddy could turn on the television, Brian and Lisa cried, "Daddy! Mother! We don't ever see you, and we can't even find ourselves in all this stuff! It was lots of fun at first, but what if we got lost in our new rooms and never found our way out? What if God can't even find us?"

Their daddy shrugged his shoulders and said, "I guess that's how it is when we try to pile up lots of stuff instead of trying to keep in touch with each other." And their mother said, "God can find us anywhere, but sometimes we forget to look for God."

*[Here are suggested questions and ideas to think about.]*

What would happen if you got a whole big truckload of toys and you couldn't even get them into the house?

What could Brian and Lisa and their mother and daddy do with all the things they had?

If you want to, you can draw a picture of Brian and Lisa and their toys. If you draw one, I'd like to see it.

**Prayer:** God, thank you for the people who love us. Thank you for our toys and clothes and games and things. Help us not to lose ourselves in the middle of them. Help us not to forget how you love us, too. We love you. Amen.

# Giving What You Have

**Purpose:** To help the children think about their own giving by telling the story of the feeding of the five thousand in a way that invites their imagining and comparing.
**Scripture:** Matthew 14:14–21.
**Materials:** None.

**Sermon:** [*Hints for telling the story: This story makes use of dialogue between Jesus and the disciples. Make the dialogue come alive with the disciple speaking conspiratorially and getting a little upset with Jesus, and the children will enjoy the story more and be drawn more fully into the experience.*]

One day Jesus was taking care of some sick people and their families and telling stories and listening to their stories. Wherever Jesus was seemed like such a good place to be that lots of people would gather around. They would listen and talk for a long time. Sometimes all day long!

On this day, Jesus and his friends were a long way from any town, and the people who came to be with them were a long way from home. Now in those days there weren't any MacDonald's or Pizza Huts or anything like that. If anyone got hungry out there, they were going to have to go a long, long way to get food.

That's what Jesus' friends were worried about: getting hungry. So they elected one man to talk to Jesus about it. He edged up through the crowd and whispered to Jesus, "Uh, Jesus, don't you think it's getting kind of, well, you know late? I mean it's like, uh, almost time for supper, and we're, I mean them, yeah, they, these people here. . . . Don't you think all these people are going to be getting hungry pretty soon? And there's just no place around here to get anything, you know? (There won't be a MacDonald's around here for nearly two thousand years!) So why don't you just wrap this up and send them home so we can—I mean they can—so that they can go  and, like, get something to eat? Okay?"

90

Jesus said (so that everyone could hear him), "They need not go anywhere. You give them something to eat!"

"SSSShh! Jesus, SShh! They'll all hear you! I don't think you understand the situation here. There are a whole lot of hungry people out there. And all we've got is about five little sandwiches and a couple of tiny sardines. And you see, we brought them along for ourselves."

"Bring what you have to me," Jesus said, "and let's see what we can do!"

"Okay, I'll do it. But I've got to warn you, Jesus, it's not even enough for me. I don't know how you expect to feed all these people here with just this. And once they smell the sardines, well. . . . Look, Jesus, I'm hungry. I mean, they are. They're hungry, you know. And there's about five thousand people out there!"

Jesus took the bread and the fish and thanked God for them. And he gave them away. And by the time he was through, everybody had enough to eat. And there were leftovers, too—twelve baskets full!

When we worship together, we remember what Jesus did when we give what we have to the offering and pray that it can be used to help other people. We don't give sandwiches and sardines or loaves and fishes, but we give what we have. And when we share the bread and wine, it's like Jesus is still with us, making sure there is enough for everybody.

*[Here are suggested ideas and questions to think about:]*

When Jesus told his friends to give what they had to the hungry people, how do you think they felt? Does anybody ever feel that way when the offering plate is passed?

Can you think of some other things we do in worship that remind us of things Jesus did?

If you were going to draw a picture about this story, what would you draw?

**Prayer:** God, thank you for the stories of Jesus and for using what we give to help others. The way you love us makes us want to give all we can because we love you, too. Amen.

# My, How You've Grown!

**Purpose:** To encourage the children in their growing faith by sharing the story of Jesus returning to his home synagogue in a way that the children can identify with and understand.
**Scripture:** Mark 6:1–6.
**Materials:** None.

**Sermon:** *[Hints for telling the story: The story begins with the identification of some feelings that you and the children may have shared. Really (gently) pinch some cheeks and pat some heads! Choose some embarrassing moment from your own childhood to substitute for the real ones from my childhood.]*
If you've ever been to a family reunion, you probably know what it feels like for someone to come up and pinch your cheeks and say, "Well, my, my! Haven't you grown?" Or, "Is that you? Why, you're such a big boy now!" Or, "My, oh my, you're such a fine little lady now!" Sometimes that can be really embarrassing.
But the most embarrassing thing is when they bring out the pictures of your diaper getting changed when you were a baby! Oh, brother! Or in the bathtub! And when they tell stories about dumb things you did that you don't even remember. (The worst one they ever tell about me is about the time my big sister tricked me into taking a bite of soap in the bathtub. Or the time I took my new pocket knife and cut the strings out of her tennis racket. How embarrassing!)
That's just what it's like when you get with people who knew you when you were a little baby. Sometimes they can really embarrass you. Not always, but sometimes. And sometimes they can really make you mad when they still treat you like a little baby or something like that. It was the same way with Jesus.
After he had already grown up and started teaching people and helping sick people and listening to people and

telling them stories, he came home for a visit. Some of his friends came along with him. Back to his old hometown! And the people there asked him to preach a sermon or something like that. So he did. And his friends probably thought he did a good job, too!

But when he was finished, somebody said, "Why, I remember when you were just a little shaver in the carpenter shop! How come you think you're so smart?" And laughed.

Somebody else said, "You're still Mary's little boy. I changed your diapers, you know. Oh, you think you're a big one now! But you're still Mary's little boy to me."

Somebody else said, "Aren't you still James' and Joses' and Judas' big brother? Remember that time they cut the strings out of your lyre? Remember that time you tricked little Joses into taking a bite of soap?"

Jesus' little sisters probably teased him. "Ooooh! Look at the big preacher man! He thinks he's so-o-o-o cool!"

And Jesus said, "It's hard to teach anybody anything when they changed your diapers!" Or something like that. And he couldn't do anything there except for helping a few sick people. They were probably new folks in town who didn't know him when he was a baby. And he just couldn't believe that his own hometown couldn't believe in him.

Didn't they know people could grow up?

*[Here are suggested ideas and questions to think about:]*

How do you think Jesus felt when he couldn't do what he wanted to do in his own hometown?

How do you think Jesus might have changed and grown while he was getting older?

How do you think you might have changed since you were a baby? Are you still changing and growing?

If you'd like to draw a picture, I'd like to see what you think you'll look like when you are all grown up. Will you stop growing and changing someday?

**Prayer:** God, thank you for loving us when we are babies, and when we do embarrassing things, and when we grow, and all the time. Help us to grow up the way you want us to, the way Jesus did. Amen.

# Learning to Love

**Purpose:** To let the children see how Jesus' disciples had to grow and learn by sharing the story of the disciples wanting to call down fire on an inhospitable Samaritan town.
**Scripture:** Luke 9:51–58.
**Materials:** None.

**Sermon:** *[Hints for telling the story: In this story, Jesus' friends are like dumb, lovable clowns. Their repetition should be the kind of thing that endears them to the children. Make it fun, not irritating. Let these friends be attractive, not distant.]*
One time Jesus and his friends were on the way to Jerusalem. As the sun was falling low and night was coming on, Jesus sent some of his friends into the village ahead of them to find them a place to stay the night. They hurried on ahead while Jesus and the other friends took their time.

When Jesus and the others were almost to the village, the friends who had gone ahead met them coming back from the town. And they were mad! "Those miserable, no-good, unfriendly, inhospitable creeps!" one of them said.

"Those dirty, miserable, no-good, unfriendly, inhospitable creeps!" added another.

"Those low-down, dirty, miserable, no-good, unfriendly, inhospitable creeps!" said a third.

"What's the matter?" Jesus asked.

"Those miserable, no-good, unfriendly, inhospitable creeps won't let us stay there!" the first one replied.

"Those dirty, miserable, no-good, unfriendly, inhospitable . . . ."

"Wait a minute!" Jesus interrupted, "Why won't they?"

"They said they don't like people who would go to Jerusalem," said one.

"And I said I don't like people who don't like people who would go to Jerusalem," said the second.

"And I said I don't like people who don't like people who don't like people who would—I mean, um, I don't like them

94

either. Those low-down, dirty, miserable. . . . "

"Hey, Jesus," another friend interrupted, "Why don't we go burn their fields?"

"No, let's burn their city," said another one.

"No, let's ask God to send down fire from heaven and burn up everything in their whole dirty, low-down, miserable, inhospitable, unfriendly. . . ."

"Hold it!" Jesus said. "When are you going to learn that we are supposed to love people? Even people who are not what we'd like them to be. Even people who don't do what we like."

"Even dirty, miserable, no-good. . ."

"Everybody," said Jesus, "even our enemies."

That night as Jesus and his friends were sitting around the campfire on the hard ground, still on their way to Jerusalem, one of Jesus' friends said, "Jesus, I'd follow you anywhere!"

And Jesus told them that foxes had holes and birds had nests but that he had nowhere to lay his head. And one of his friends said, "And it's all because of those miserable, no-good, unfriendly, inhospitable creeps!"

"Haven't you learned yet?" Jesus sighed. "I love them, too."

And Jesus' friends just stared at the fire. They had a lot to learn.

*[Here are suggested ideas and questions to think about: ]*

If you were already a grown-up, could you still grow?

Did Jesus really love people who weren't nice to him? How do you know?

What kind of people did Jesus try to help learn and grow?

If you'd like to draw a picture of some animals in their homes and Jesus with no home, I'd like to see it. Or if you can imagine what a home for Jesus might look like and what kind of people might be there, that would be nice, too.

**Prayer:** God, thank you for loving us even when we are not nice to each other. Thank you for helping us learn and grow, no matter how old we are. Amen.

# Taking Care of Others First

**Purpose:** To help the children understand how important it was to Jesus to take care of others first and oneself second by telling the story of Peter's reaction to Jesus' prediction of his death.

**Scripture:** Matthew 16:21–25.

**Materials:** None.

**Sermon:** *[Hints for telling the story: Don't try to make this a story with a moral: Always take care of others before yourself. It's really an invitation to share a moment with Jesus and his disciples in which we see how important caring for others was for Jesus. Play the role of Peter with more compassion than humor this time. He's really trying to take care of Jesus, after all.]*

Jesus once told his friends that, the way things were going, it looked like he was going to get into a lot of trouble. He was headed for Jerusalem, and there were lots of people there who didn't like Jesus. They didn't like what he was saying. They didn't like what he was doing. And they didn't like the way so many other people liked him!

The people who didn't like Jesus and the things he was saying and doing were getting ready to make him pay. Jesus told his friends that, if he didn't stop, when he got to Jerusalem those people would even try to have him killed. And as it turned out, they did!

But when Jesus was saying this, one of Jesus' friends, whose name was Peter, told Jesus that it didn't have to happen that way. He didn't think Jesus had to keep on saying things and doing things that would get him in such big trouble. He liked Jesus very much, and he wanted him to be happy and not get hurt. And not get into trouble. And certainly not get killed! He thought that Jesus should just take care of himself and be happy. And he told Jesus what he thought.

Poor Jesus! Sometimes his friends just didn't understand! Remember that time they wanted to burn a whole village because they didn't offer them a place to stay? Jesus had been showing his friends, in every way he could think of, that they ought to look out for other people instead of looking out for themselves. He had been showing them and telling them in every way that helping other people and loving them was much more important than anything. It was more important than rules. It was more important than having fun. Or anything else. And now Peter was telling Jesus not to keep on taking care of other people with his stories and his listening and his helping people. Peter was telling Jesus to look out for "Number One," to take care of himself first!

Jesus said to Peter, "I don't know where you get your ideas! But it's certainly not from me!" Or something like that. And he explained it all one more time: "People who are going to be my friends and live my way are going to have to learn to look out for other people first and themselves second! That's the very best way to take care of yourself anyway: Take care of other people. It will make you happier than anything else! It will make your life worth living. Even if it gets you into trouble sometimes. Even if people get mad at you sometimes. Even if they don't understand what you're trying to do."

Taking care of other people is the best way to take care of yourself. Giving happiness is the best way to get happiness. That's what Jesus thought. But Peter and Jesus' other friends still had a lot to learn about that. So do we.

[Here are suggested ideas and questions to think about:]

Who was Peter trying to take care of, himself or Jesus? Why?

What do you think would happen if you took care of someone else first and then took care of yourself? Do you know anyone who does that?

I'm not sure what kind of picture you can draw about this story. Maybe a picture about you taking care of someone else. Whatever picture you draw, I'd like to see it.

**Prayer**: God, thank you for always taking care of us first. You're the greatest at that, and we love you. Amen.

# Many Ways of Helping

**Purpose:** To invite children to consider the many ways they can help others by sharing with them the story of Jesus' visit with Mary and Martha.
**Scripture:** Luke 10:38–41.
**Materials:** None.

**Sermon:** *[Hints for telling the story: The repetition in this story will make it more fun and easier to listen to. Try to make the children feel at home in the story by using it.]*
When Jesus and his friends were traveling around their homeland helping sick people get well, telling stories, and listening to the stories of the people, they often came to the town where two sisters lived. Their names were Mary and Martha.

One time when Jesus came to stay at Mary and Martha's house, Martha probably spent time cooking and cleaning and making the house just right. She was probably a very good cook, and she probably made Jesus feel very comfortable when he stayed with her by the careful way she cooked and prepared.

Meanwhile, her sister Mary sat down and listened to Jesus teach and tell stories. She was probably a very good listener, and she probably made Jesus feel very comfortable when he was talking to her by the careful way she listened.

Martha had lots of cooking and cleaning to do. She really liked for Jesus to be in her home, but maybe this time something went wrong. Maybe she burned the special dinner she was cooking. Or maybe she spilled some soup she'd been cooking for hours. Or maybe she remembered something she needed when it was too late to go and get it. Those things happened to cooks a long time ago just like they happen today.

Whatever it was, Martha was upset. And she saw Mary, not worrying at all, just sitting there listening to Jesus like there was nothing going on in the kitchen or anywhere else in the house or anyplace else in the city or anyplace else in the whole world! And she saw Jesus just sitting there talking to Mary and the other friends just like there was nothing going on in the kitchen or anywhere else in the house or anyplace else in the city or anyplace else in the whole world!

Martha was upset, probably because everything didn't work out like she planned and it seemed that no one else cared. She went into the room where Jesus and Mary and the others were. And she said, "Jesus, here you are sitting and talking like there's nothing going on in the kitchen or anywhere else in the house or anyplace else in the city or anyplace else in the world, and Mary's sitting in here doing the same thing. Don't you care that she's left all the work for me to do? Tell her to come and help me!"

Martha probably wasn't really upset with Jesus or Mary or any of Jesus' friends. But you know how sometimes when things go wrong: You end up acting like you're upset with people you love. Jesus probably knew that, too. He didn't say, "Well, it's not my fault Mary's sitting in here! I didn't chain her to the chair or anything. You tell her yourself if you're so upset about it!"

He said, "Martha! Martha! You are helping me and my friends in the way that you like best, and Mary is helping us in her way, too. There are lots of ways to help people. Your way and Mary's way are very important, and nobody can take anything away from either of you." Or something like that.

There are lots and lots of ways to help others. One way is to cook for them. One way is to really listen to them. One way is to tell them stories. One way is to help them get well. One way is to eat what they have cooked for you. One way is to thank them for everything they do for you. One way is to— well, like I said, there are lots of ways. You probably know as many as I do.

One important thing to remember about helping others is that there are lots of ways to do it. And my way may not be the same as your way. Just like Mary's was not the same as Martha's.

*[Here are suggested ideas and questions to think about: ]*

What are some ways you know to let me know you're

really listening to the stories I tell you? (It really helps to know you're listening.)

What are some ways you can help other people feel at home when we worship together?

If you want to, you can draw a picture of Mary or Martha or you or me trying to help someone else. I'd like to see what you draw us doing.

**Prayer:** God, we know so many ways to help others. Help us not to get stuck doing one thing all the time. Help us not to think our ways are the only ways. Thank you for all the ways Jesus knew to help people. Amen.

# The Treasure Field

**Purpose:** To share the discovery of a special place that is the source of good feelings and good stories for generations (a place like the kingdom of heaven or like the Bible) by sharing a reshaping of a parable Jesus told.
**Scripture:** Matthew 13:44.
**Materials:** None.

**Sermon:** *[Hints for telling the story: Let some of your own warm feelings for such a treasured place show through your description of this place. Let the story take the children there with you in their imaginations.]*
Once upon a time there was a little girl who went on a picnic with her grandparents. After they ate lunch, the little girl (I think her name was Lisa) went for a walk in a nearby field. She saw lots of wonderful things there: birds of all kinds singing their merry songs, a family of rabbits hiding in the grass, hopping crickets, wildflowers, and green, green grass. There was even a pond in the field that was clear and cool with croaking frogs and splashing fish. There were places to walk and places to climb and places to hide and places to sit and places to run and places to jump. It seemed like the most wonderful place in the world!
It seemed like no time before she heard her grandmother calling, "Lisa! Lisa! Come on back now. It's time to go home." Lisa felt like she had found a new home in the wonderful field. But she skipped back to her grandmother's side and said, "Oh, Grandmother! In this field is the most wonderful treasure! I want to come back here again and again."
Her grandmother said, "We will, dear."
"Can we come back tomorrow?" Lisa asked.
"If you want, dear," said her grandmother.
Every day for the rest of her visit, Lisa and her grandparents would go back to the "Treasure Field," as Lisa began to call it. They even went one day when it was raining and just sat in the car and looked out the window.

101

"Grandfather," Lisa said, "you know what I'd like more than anything else in the whole world?"

"What, dear?" her grandfather asked.

"I'd like to build a house and live in the Treasure Field."

When Lisa went home, all she talked about was the Treasure Field. Her parents didn't understand why. Her friends got tired of listening to her. Her big brother teased her. Whenever she walked into the room, he would say, "Ladies and gentlemen, I present The Queen of Trash Your Field!" And he and his friends would laugh. They didn't understand.

But it didn't matter to Lisa. She had found a wonderful treasure, and she wanted to be there in the field more than anything else. She drew pictures of the animals and wrote stories about the birds. Underneath her bed was a very quiet place that reminded her of a place in the field under the low limbs of a juniper bush. She crawled under there often and pretended she was back in her Treasure Field.

When Lisa grew up she became a minister (just like me), and she told lots of stories to children and grown-ups. When she told them how much God loved them, she told them about how much her grandparents loved her and how they took her to the Treasure Field again and again. She told them about how hard it was to follow God's way sometimes. She told them about how hard it was when her brother teased her about the Treasure Field. When she told them how Bible stories could give them exciting adventures to imagine and places to dream of and secret hiding places to find, she told them about the Treasure Field.

More than anything else, the Treasure Field was her place. And even when she grew up, she would go there on vacation sometimes. And she took her children to visit sometimes, even after her grandparents didn't live there anymore. And one day someone turned the Treasure Field into a parking lot for a big shopping center. But Lisa still remembered it and told its stories. And so did her children. And her children's children. And her children's children's children. And so do I.

*[Here are suggested ideas and questions to think about: ]*

Have you ever been somewhere like the Treasure Field?

Can you imagine what your own Treasure Field would be like? If you want to draw a picture of one, I'd really like to see it.

Jesus told a story about a man who found a great treasure in a field. Maybe you and your family can find the story and find out what the man did.

**Prayer:** God, thank you for places like Lisa's Treasure Field, places where we can remember and pretend, places where we can feel at home, places where we can be very happy. And thank you for stories that can take us to treasure fields. Amen.

# Loving by the Rules

**Purpose:** To suggest using the Bible as a source of ways to love, not just rules, by sharing a story about Jesus showing more interest in helping people than in rules.

**Scripture:** Luke 14:1–6.

**Materials:** None.

**Sermon:** [Hints for telling the story: Use your voice to introduce the Pharisees as Jesus' enemies in this story. The role they play will do more to explain who they are than the verbal explanations, but the verbal explanations will help the older children understand a little more.]

One time Jesus and his friends were eating dinner at the home of a Pharisee. There were lots of Pharisees there, too. And they were watching Jesus to see what he would do. The Pharisees were very curious about Jesus because they cared very much about their Bible and the rules for living they found in it. Jesus taught people about the Bible and about rules and about living, and the Pharisees were watching to see what he would do and what he would say.

Some of the Pharisees did not like what Jesus taught. And they were always watching to see if Jesus would make a mistake or do something wrong. They hoped to catch him doing something wrong and show everyone that they knew more about God's way than he did.

That night at dinner, they had their chance. A sick man came right in to the dinner table and asked Jesus to help him. The Pharisees stopped eating and looked up at Jesus. One of them whispered to the one sitting beside him, "Now, let's see what he'll do with this."

The other one whispered back, "We'll catch him this time." They smiled and watched.

The reason they were watching so closely was because there was a rule about keeping the Sabbath day holy. And this was the Sabbath day. And on that day, in order to keep it holy, people were supposed to rest and do no work at all.

Now, the sick man was asking Jesus to help him. Was it work to help him? If it was, would Jesus be breaking the rules?

Jesus looked at the Pharisees and said, "Is it against the rules to help a sick person on the Sabbath or not?" He knew what they were thinking. They didn't say anything out loud, but one of them whispered, "He's the one who has to answer that one. If he helps the sick man, he'll be working. If he doesn't help him, he can't say he loves everybody."

Jesus didn't even worry about it. He helped the man get well and sent him on his way. It didn't matter if it was work or not. To the Pharisees who didn't like Jesus, it didn't matter if the poor sick man was now happy and well or not.

"He worked!" they wanted to say. "You saw him! He broke the rules! Oh boy, he's in trouble now! We got him this time! Jesus worked on the Sabbath!"

Jesus looked at them and said, "Which one of you would not help your own son if he needed you on the Sabbath day?"

They didn't know what to say. Of course they would help their own sons.

"Which one of you would not help your cow that was stuck in the mud to get out if it happened on the Sabbath day?"

They didn't know what to say. Of course they would take care of their own cows. But rules were rules. And a teacher like Jesus was supposed to go by the rules. Especially the rules of the Bible!

But Jesus didn't think rules were rules. Jesus thought people were people, and God was God, and love was love. And loving God and loving people and taking care of them and helping them were more important than any rules. Jesus thought that if there was any important rule in the whole Bible, that was it: Love God and love other people.

I think so, too.

*[Here are suggested ideas and questions to think about: ]*

If your own brother were sick and needed help very much on a school day, would you help him? What about your own mother? What if there was a rule that everyone had to go to school, no matter what?

Have you ever gotten into trouble for doing the right

thing?

How does telling Bible stories help us to help people?

Can you think of any other Bible stories about helping people? If you can think of one, draw a picture of it. If you do, I'd really like to see it.

**Prayer:** God, thank you for the rules and stories of the Bible. Please help us to always listen to them in order to hear ways we can help people and love them. Thank you for always loving us, even when we don't help as much as we could. Amen.

## Everyone Is Important

**Purpose:** To introduce the idea of treating everyone as important by sharing the story of Jesus noticing and healing a sick woman.
**Scripture:** Mark 5:21–43.
**Materials:** None.

**Sermon:** *[Hints for telling the story: Use your voice to create characters and mood. As you tell of the woman working her way through the crowd, use body language to act out her movements. When the woman comes out of the crowd, talk very fast and with great emotion.]*
One time a very important man came up to Jesus and his friends and fell down on his knees in front of Jesus. Well, you can imagine that everyone around wondered what was going on when they saw that. A crowd gathered around Jesus and his friends and the very important man, whose name was Jairus. Jairus said to Jesus, "My little daughter is very, very sick. And she may even die! Please come and help her get well. Please!"

Jesus helped Jairus get up and went with him right away. And the crowd followed along. All the people squeezed close together. They wanted to see what would happen next, and they wanted to hear what Jesus and Jairus were talking about along the way.

One woman in the crowd was very sick. She had been sick for twelve years, and she wasn't getting any better. She had been to lots of doctors and had taken lots of medicine, but she could not get well. She had heard that Jesus helped sick people get well, and she was hoping to find some way to talk to him or even touch him. She thought that Jesus was so special that if she could touch him she would be well.

But that was a problem. You see, in those days, it was against the rules for men even to talk to women in public. Except their wives. And it was really against the rules for men to touch sick women. If that happened, the man had to go to

107

the temple and pray and wash himself over and over. Just for touching a sick woman.

But now was the woman's chance! Everybody in the crowded street was so close together that they were touching everybody else and nobody was even noticing. If she could get close enough to Jesus to touch him, she knew she would start feeling better right away. She pushed a little here and ducked under an arm there and squeezed through here and wriggled through there. She could hear Jesus talking to Jairus. She pushed a little more and ducked under another arm and squeezed and wriggled through some more tight places. She could see Jesus! With a little more pushing and a little more ducking and a little more squeezing and a little more wriggling, she could reach out and touch Jesus. And she did! And she started feeling better just like she knew she would.

But suddenly Jesus and Jairus stopped. The whole crowd stopped. And Jesus said, "Who touched me?" His friends thought maybe he was joking. They said, "In this crowd, you ask who touched you?"

The woman thought, "Oh, he noticed me. Now he's going to have to go to the temple and wash and pray. He won't be able to help the little girl. Now he's going to be really mad. But I had to do it! There was no other way."

She stepped out of the crowd and fell down at Jesus' feet. Everybody was so quiet they could hear her crying softly. Jesus knelt down. Maybe he put his hand on her shoulder, and the crowd gasped. Maybe the people who didn't like him rubbed their hands together and said, "He touched her! And everybody saw him do it! Oh boy, oh boy, he broke the rules, and now everybody will see that he's not so great!"

The woman told Jesus the whole story and how sorry she was and how she thought she could just touch him and get well. And she was! But she cried and cried. Jesus took her hand. He helped her stand up. And he spoke to her. "Daughter," he said, "your faith has made you well; go in peace. Get well and help others do the same." Or something like that.

But just then one of Jairus' servants came up and told him his daughter was dead. And they didn't need to bother Jesus anymore. But Jesus hadn't forgotten the sick little girl.

You and your family can find the rest of the story in your Bible. It's Mark 5:35-42.

*[Here are suggested ideas and questions to think about: ]*
What do you think Jesus' friends thought about all this?
Was the woman Jesus helped important? How can you tell whether someone is important or not?
If you find the rest of the story in your Bible, you can draw a picture of the ending of the story. If you do, I'd like to see it very much.

**Prayer:** God, thank you for always noticing us, even when there are lots of other important things to be done. Thank you for making us important. We love you. Amen.

# Time to Be Alone

**Purpose:** To alert children to their own need to find quiet "alone time" for sharing their feelings by telling the story of Jesus and his friends expressing their sadness at the death of John.
**Scripture:** Mark 6:30–34.
**Materials:** None.

**Sermon:** *[Hints for telling the story: Like the story of the Treasure Field (See Pentecost #14), this is a gentle story that invites the children to come and share the sadness of Jesus and his friends. Speak carefully and be attentive to the responses.]*
The day that Jesus heard the news that his cousin John had died, he was very sad, and so were his friends. Some of them helped to bury John, and after that they came back to where Jesus and the others were. They told Jesus about the place where they buried John and about how he died.

Like his cousin Jesus, John was always getting into trouble with those people who were jealous of his popularity and did not want to follow his teaching. Finally, one of them had ordered that John be put in prison so he would stop his preaching and teaching. Then they ordered that John's head be cut off. It was a terrible way to die. It made Jesus and his friends sad that John was dead. It made them sad to think that Jesus might someday be killed like his cousin. It made them sad to think that they themselves might die someday. It made them all very sad.

They didn't pretend that they were not sad. They didn't try not to cry. They didn't try to stay busy or keep on working. Jesus said, "Let's go away by ourselves to a lonely place and rest awhile." And they got into a boat and headed for just such a place. And I suppose that while they were there, they were going to tell the stories they remembered about John. And sometimes they would laugh, and sometimes they would cry. And sometimes they would just be very, very quiet. And sometimes they would pray. Maybe they would thank God for John's life. Maybe they would pray for John's family. Maybe they would pray for themselves.

Jesus knew that the best way to be happy was to make other people happy. But he also knew that sometimes you have to be alone. Sometimes you have to take care of yourself and your own feelings. Sometimes you have to be very quiet and still. Sometimes you have to cry. Sometimes you have to get away with just your very best friends. So when they heard the sad news about John's death, Jesus and his friends headed for a lonely place.

When they got to the lonely place, Jesus and his friends found a lot of lonely people there. They had found out where Jesus and his friends were going, and they got there first. From all the towns around, they came to see Jesus and hear him talk and share their stories and help sick people get well.

Jesus just couldn't turn them away, even though he was very sad. Even though he needed to be alone with his friends. The people looked lonely, too. They looked like sheep who didn't have a shepherd or anyone to take care of them, and show them where the water was, and scare off the animals that hunted them, and take them to where there was new grass. They needed someone to take care of them. So Jesus did. And some other times and other days, Jesus took time to be alone and take care of himself.

Everybody has to do that sometime.

*[Here are suggested ideas and questions to think about: ]*

Have you ever had someone you love die? Were you sad?

What do you do when you are sad?

Do you have a lonely place you can go when you need to take care of yourself?

If you want to draw a picture about this story, one good one might be a picture of the lonely place to which Jesus and his friends were going.

**Prayer:** God, thank you for being with us when we are sad and when we are happy. Help us all to take time to find lonely places for being quiet and taking care of ourselves. Help us to take time to listen and not just talk. Amen.

# Who Do You Say That I Am?

**Purpose:** To encourage the children to consider their own response to the stories of Jesus by sharing with them the story of Peter's confession.
**Scripture:** Matthew 16:13–20.
**Materials:** None.

**Sermon:** *[Hints for telling the story: Let the silence waiting for an answer to Jesus' question last. Let the uneasiness be felt.]*
Once Jesus and his friends were sitting talking to one another. As usual, they were telling stories to one another. And Jesus was listening to their stories and telling stories of his own. As usual, they sometimes seemed to understand what Jesus was talking about. And sometimes it seemed like they would never get it right.

They were talking about the way God was working to take care of the world and the way God was trying to show everyone how they were loved. They were talking about someone whom many of their favorite stories said was coming. The stories said this coming one would show everyone God's love once and for all. The stories said this coming one would be called the Son of man.

There were all kinds of stories about the Son of man. Almost every one of them said that the Son of man was coming someday to show God's people what God was like and what God wanted. But there were lots of different stories about who the Son of man was going to be. He was sort of a mystery. Everyone was hoping he would come, but no one was sure when he would come or who he would be when he did.

You can imagine how much fun it was to tell the stories and talk about who the Son of man might be or when he might show up. That day, Jesus asked his friends who people were saying the Son of man was. They had all kinds of answers: "Some people say the Son of man is your cousin John, the one they call John the Baptizer." Remember how sad Jesus and his friends were when John was killed? "I've heard people say that the Son of man will be that old prophet Elijah who lived a long time ago. They say he may come back again!" "Well, I heard he was going to be Jeremiah or some other prophet. But not Elijah!"

It was fun to talk about the different stories and argue about which one might be right, and all Jesus' friends had lots of stories and ideas. But Jesus didn't really want to know more stories that day. He knew most of their stories already. What Jesus really wanted to know was what his friends thought themselves. Not what they had heard other people say. Not what somebody else's story said. So he asked them, "What about you? Who do you say that I am?"

Well, that was different! That was really getting personal. They couldn't just show off about what they had heard. They had to say what they really thought. And not just about anything! About what they really thought about their friend Jesus. They were very quiet. One friend looked at another. and another looked at another, and nobody said anything at all. One of the friends looked up at the clouds. Another looked at his sandals. One looked at a bird singing in a nearby tree. Nobody said anything.

One started whistling. Jesus just waited. *[Quietly wait in silence.]*

Finally, one of the friends named Peter decided he would tell Jesus what he really thought. Everyone else was sitting quietly. Peter said, "You are the one we're all waiting for. You are the one who is showing us God's way, the Son of man. You are the Christ, the Son of the living God."

Jesus smiled. He was pleased that Peter had made up his mind. He was pleased that Peter understood. "Good for you," he said. "That's an idea you didn't get out of nowhere. I think you got it from God."

Jesus' friends all had to make up their minds about Jesus. They all had to decide what they thought about him. They all had to decide what they were going to do and say about the things Jesus taught them. That day Peter really seemed to decide. But he had to decide again and again on

113

other days. And he didn't always decide the same thing.

We have to make up our minds, too. We can't just tell stories about Jesus and say what other people think. We can't listen to what other people say. But if we listen and pray, God will find a way to let us know the way. Just like God did with Peter.

**Prayer:** God, thank you for all the stories about Jesus and all the stories about the way you love us. Help us to listen carefully to all the stories. And help us to decide what we will say about you and do for you. We love you. Amen.

# Jeremiah

**Purpose:** To let the children know that God doesn't call people to do easy things and that it's acceptable to be angry with God by sharing some of the story of the prophet Jeremiah.
**Scripture:** Jeremiah 20:7–13.
**Materials:** None.

**Sermon:** [*Hints for telling the story: When Jeremiah yells, yell! When Jeremiah pouts, pout! Help the children get acquainted with this character as someone very interesting and real! Someone Jesus must have liked a lot.*]
This is a story that Jesus listened to when he was a boy. It's about Jeremiah, who was one of God's people. Sometimes Jeremiah knew just what God would want him to do. And sometimes he wasn't so sure.

The people in the town where Jeremiah lived really started doing things that Jeremiah knew God didn't like. They were mean to each other. They hurt other people. They didn't seem to pay any attention to God at all. When those things happened, Jeremiah just couldn't keep quiet. He felt like God was really telling him to say something. He felt like God was really hurt and angry about what was going on. So he said, "Stop this! Stop being mean! Stop hurting people! Stop forgetting God! You're going to make God really angry! And you'll be sorry if you do!"

Do you think anybody liked it when Jeremiah said that? They didn't.

Do you think anybody cheered and said, "Yea, Jeremiah!"? They didn't.

Do you think anybody said, "Good idea, Jeremiah. You're right!"? They didn't.

Do you think anybody got mad? Sure they did. And they threw Jeremiah in jail.

Then Jeremiah was mad. He was mad at the people, and he was mad at God.

115

He said, "God, I thought I knew what you wanted me to do. I made up my mind, and then I did it. And look what happened! Every time I speak, people laugh at me. Even my close friends think I'm crazy! Maybe I should just be quiet.

"Maybe I should just make up my mind to forget you and stop trying to say what I think you want me to say. Maybe I should just make up my mind to stop trying to do what you want me to do. Yeah, maybe then I wouldn't have anybody laughing at me.

"Maybe then my friends would be my friends again. Maybe then I wouldn't be in jail."

Jeremiah decided it would be a lot easier to let God take care of things without him. But then he remembered that he had had that idea before.

He said to God, "Every time I decide that, before I can even feel good for a second, you start getting to me again! I start noticing how people are mean to each other and how they hurt each other. And I start feeling terrible about not saying anything. And I feel worse and worse. I feel even worse than I do now. And I do it again! I say, 'You people better start remembering God. If you don't . . . .' There I go again. God, it's not easy to make up my mind about you. Sometimes I wish you'd leave me alone. Sometimes I wish I had never been born! It's just too hard to try to be one of your people!"

The things God wants us to do aren't always easy. They aren't always fun. Sometimes they are different from what other people are doing. Sometimes people who speak out for God get into trouble. Like Jeremiah! Like Jesus' cousin, John the Baptizer.

Like Jesus. It's a good thing God sticks with us even when we feel bad. Even when we're mad. Even when it's God that we're mad at! That's one of the things that helps us keep on deciding to stick with God. God always sticks with us.

*[Here are suggested ideas and questions to think about: ]*
Do you think Jesus remembered this story when he grew up? How can you tell?

What do you think God thinks when we get mad at God?

How do you think God can still love us when we're mad?

Can you think of anything God might want you to do that isn't easy?

If you want to, you can draw a picture of Jeremiah in jail. You'll have to decide whether to draw him mad or happy. Sometimes he was one, and sometimes he was the other. Like we are.

**Prayer:** God, thank you for loving us even when we make up our minds not to listen to you. Even when we're mad at you. We won't stay mad for long because we really do love you. Amen.

# The Armor of God

**Purpose:** To introduce children to the idea of God's way being different from the way of toymakers and soldiers by sharing the idea of God's armor.
**Scripture:** Ephesians 6:10–20.
**Materials:** None.

**Sermon:** *[Hints for telling the story: There is very little narrative here, but you can still invite the children to participate in your imaginings if you share a sense of discovery and mystery with them. That should be the tone: discovery, not explanations.]*
I saw a toy once that was supposed to be especially for boys and girls who were friends of Jesus. It was a plastic sword and a scabbard to keep the sword in, and a belt to put it around your waist. I think there was even a plastic helmet to wear and armor for your chest so that you would look like a real soldier in shining armor. Even if you were just pretending. Even if you were just wearing plastic armor and carrying a plastic sword and a plastic shield.

The people who made the toy plastic armor called it "God's armor." If they hadn't called it "God's armor," or if they hadn't said it was especially for boys and girls who were friends of Jesus, I probably would never have noticed it at all. There are a lot of toys I don't notice. But since they called it "God's armor," I started wondering what kind of armor God would want you to wear. I started wondering about whether or not God would want us to have shields and swords and things like that.

In my Bible I found a letter written not too long after Jesus died. It was a letter written to some Christians who lived in those days. They were days when soldiers carried shields and swords and wore helmets and sometimes armor, too. In one part, the letter said, "Put on all the armor of God!" In those days, there were soldiers who used their swords to put Christians in jail. There were even some soldiers who killed

Christians. It was a time when Christians really needed armor or something. They needed protection from soldiers and from shields and helmets and swords and armor.

So, the letter told Christians to put on God's armor, the armor that God would give them. It made me wonder what kind of armor God would give people. If God wanted Christians to love each other, what kind of armor would God give? I kept on reading the letter. It turns out it wasn't really armor at all they were talking about. It was something else. Here's just about what the letter said:

Instead of an armored belt, tell the truth.

Instead of armor on your chest, stick close to God.

Instead of armored shoes, tell about God's way of peace.

Instead of a shield, carry faith.

Instead of a helmet, wear God's love to save you.

Instead of a sword, use words about God and God's way.

To get ready for those soldiers who will attack you, pray.

Never give up!

That's the way Jesus taught his friends to put on armor. By not putting on any real armor at all. But by putting God's ways all over their lives and around themselves. Not by fighting and killing with swords and armor and shields. But by loving and talking and praying.

Remember how Jesus' friends didn't understand him all the time? Remember how they wanted to burn down a village where the people didn't give them a place to stay the night? Remember how they didn't know what to say about Jesus? It took them a long time to understand. Us, too. Jesus' friends still have trouble knowing what Jesus wants us to do. It's not easy. I have trouble myself knowing what to say about Jesus. And I think those people who thought God's armor was a shield and a sword and a helmet and a scabbard and a belt really didn't understand. That's not God's armor; that's a soldier's armor. That's not what Jesus' friends wore; that's what soldiers wore who killed Jesus' friends.

Here's what God's armor looks like. *[Hold up nothing.]* You can't see it. Just like you can't see God. You can only see people telling the truth, sticking close to God, telling about God's ways, remembering God's love, listening for God's word, praying, and never giving up. That's the only kind of armor for Christian boys and girls. Just like God is the only kind of God for us, too.

At least that's the way I understand what Jesus taught us!

*[Here are suggested ideas and questions to think about:]*
What difference does it make what toys you play with?

Does God's armor keep all bad things from happening to God's people?

Do you know anyone who understands everything about God and Jesus?

Can you draw a picture of a soldier wearing a soldier's armor and one of Jesus' friends wearing God's armor? What will they be doing? If you decide to draw a picture, I hope you will show it to me later.

**Prayer:** God, sometimes we really want to be your people, but we don't understand how. Help us never to give up trying to do things your way, the way Jesus taught us. Amen.

## How Sad the Ways of War!

**Purpose:** To acquaint children with the sadness of war by sharing with them the story of Absalom's death.
**Scripture:** 2 Samuel 18:1, 5, 9–15, 24–33.
**Materials:** None.

**Sermon:** *[Hints for telling the story: Let the waiting build tension. Let the sadness be real.]*
When Jesus was a boy, people told him stories about King David and what a great soldier David was. After he got started by killing the giant Goliath, he led his armies to many victories. The stories about King David's armies make us think that whenever he went to battle, there were great victories and glorious celebrations. They make us think that going to war is a great adventure. Sometimes they even make us think that going to war would be fun. But wars are never fun.

One time King David's army went to war against the armies of King David's son whose name was Absalom. King David was ready to lead the fight against the enemy. Even when the enemy leader was his own son. He divided his army into three groups and put a brave general in charge of each one. And King David said, "I will lead the charge myself."

His generals didn't think that was a good idea. They reminded David that when armies went to war, many people died. They reminded him that he might be killed himself. They told him that it would be better for him to stay in the city. "I will do whatever you think best," the king said. "But watch out for my son Absalom. Don't let anyone kill him!"

All day King David paced up and down in the city waiting for news of the battle. All day he worried about his armies. But mostly he worried about his son, Absalom. He was more worried about his enemy who was also his son than anything else. Because King David loved his son, his enemy, Absalom.

It was not a glorious day for David's armies that day. It was a horrible and sad day for David's armies and for the enemy armies of the king's son, Absalom. At the end of the fighting, twenty thousand men had been killed on the battle-field. And in the forest surrounding the battlefield, even more people were killed. And in the cities of King David and the cities of his son, his enemy, Absalom, there were twenty thousand families waiting to hear the news of the battle. The families were waiting to hear if their sons and brothers and fathers were killed on the battlefield. They were waiting to hear if their sons and brothers and fathers were killed in the forest.

King David was in the city waiting, too. King David was waiting at the city wall for news of the battle. He was looking for a messenger. He watched and waited all day long. He paced back and forth and watched and waited. At last, far, far away, the king saw someone coming. It looked like a messenger on the way. "Look!" he said, "A messenger is bringing news of the battle."

The messenger came running. King David thought that he would never get there. But finally he arrived, breathing hard. "Praise the Lord, your God, who has given your armies victory over your enemy!" he cried. But King David did not even listen to the news. "Is my son Absalom all right?" he asked. The messenger did not know because he had hurried to be the first one to bring the good news of the glorious victory to the king.

King David was already looking for another messenger who could tell him the news he was really worried about. The news about Absalom, his son, his enemy, whom he loved. Finally, another messenger arrived. "I have good news for Your Majesty!" he said, "Your army has won a great victory!"

"But what about my son Absalom? Is he all right?" the king asked.

The messenger shook his head and told the king how Absalom had been killed. King David went to his room and cried and cried and cried. And twenty thousand fathers and mothers and sisters and brothers and sons and daughters went to their rooms and cried and cried and cried, too.

The glorious victory did not seem glorious at all. The good news of the victory seemed like terrible news to the families of those who were killed. And whenever people heard the story of that glorious victory, they remembered the great sadness of the king who loved his enemy, his son, Absalom. And they remembered the great sadness of the families of all the soldiers who had been killed that day.

And maybe we should remember, too, whenever we start thinking that war might be a great adventure or whenever we start thinking about glorious fighting. Oh, there are glorious stories and glorious victories sometimes. But there is always a terrible, terrible sadness. For kings and soldiers and everyone who goes to war.

*[Here are suggested ideas and questions to think about:]*

What do you think would happen if everyone remembered how sad wars are instead of how exciting they are?

What would you do if you were very sad because someone you loved died?

Some kids like to draw pictures of battles and armies. Instead of something like that, I wonder if you could draw a picture of someone who is really sad. We can talk about how to help someone like that if we look at your picture.

**Prayer:** God, thank you for the brave people who go to war against their enemies even when they know how sad war is. And thank you for the brave people who will not go to war because they know how much sadness it always brings. Amen.

# C. Creation: God's Gift

*Patrice L. Rosner*

The story of creation, the first story in the Bible, sets the stage for all of history and begins the drama of the covenant relationship between God and all else. Although young children cannot relate to historical events, and though they often image God as a bearded man, the creation event is full of other ideas and images of God appropriate for children ages four to eight.

Young children can begin to grasp the idea that the world is a gift from God. Many passages in the Bible, such as Isaiah 45:18-19, declare that God created the earth for good and for a place where humans can live. Because they are learning from parents and guardians that gifts are to be cared for, they may be able to grasp the idea of caring for God's gift of the world. As children begin to take on more responsibilities at home, such as making their beds, straightening their rooms, folding handkerchiefs and towels in the laundry, setting and clearing the table, and caring for pets, they are learning to be partners in the care of God's world.

These three sermons offer an opportunity to help children praise the beauty of God's creation, identify the dependability of God, and describe our responsibility as stewards of the gift.

## All Things Bright and Beautiful

**Purpose:** To praise God for the beauty of creation.
**Scripture:** Genesis 1:1—2:3.
**Materials:** Bible; flannel board with cutouts for the six days of creation; hymnbook with the hymn "All Things Bright and Beautiful."

**Sermon:** *[An important part of this sermon is the children's participation in making the picture on the flannel board. Each child needs a chance to add at least one piece to the picture. In this way, they help create the story. Do not read this story from the Bible, but hold a Bible in your lap and show the children where Genesis is found.]*
The very first story in our Bible is the story of God creating the world. We are not told exactly how God did this, only that when God spoke things happened. At first, everything was covered with water and was dark and confused so God said "Let there be light" and there was light. God saw that the light was good. God called the light Day and the darkness God called Night. *[After you describe each day, ask one of the children to add an appropriate representation to the dark-colored flannel board. For the first day, cover the left half with white or yellow fabric.]* Sometimes we're scared in the dark, but we know that God has made light so the dark is not quite so scary.
After an evening and a morning, God divided the waters so there was a sky. God saw that this was good. *[Add blue fabric for the sky.]*
Then God said, "Let some of this water below the sky be gathered together in one place so there can be some dry land." God called the dry land Earth and the waters God called the Sea. Plants and trees started to grow on the earth. God was happy about creation. The Bible tells us that God saw that each part was good. *[Add green and brown fabric for the earth and more blue fabric for the seas.]*
After the evening and the morning, God made lights for

125

the day and the night. What lights the sky in the daytime? What lights the sky at night? *[Add a sun, moon, and stars.]* Have you ever gone outside on a clear night and looked up at the stars? God has made hundreds and hundreds of stars. They seem to twinkle all over the sky. They are beautiful. And God saw that it was good. *[Encourage the children to join in this refrain with you by repeating the phrase once or twice.]*

After another evening and morning, God decorated the sky and the seas by making lots of different kinds of birds and lots of different kinds of sea animals. *[Add birds and fish to the flannel board.]* Name one kind of bird God made. *[Let the children respond.]* How about a fish? *[Pause for response.]* Birds and fish come in all colors and sizes and shapes. If they were all the same, that would be boring, but the differences are beautiful. And we know that God saw that this was good. *[Invite the congregation to repeat with the children.]* "God saw that this was good."

Well, there was another evening and another morning and then God made lots of other kinds of animals, like cows and bugs and elephants and monkeys. What is your favorite animal? What, do you think, is the funniest animal? *[Add animals to the flannel board.]* What do you suppose God thought of all this? Let's say it together: "God saw that this was good."

Now that there was day and night, sky, earth, and seas, sun, moon, and stars, birds, fish, and all other animals, God created people. Like the birds, fish, and other animals, people are different too. Some are tall; some are short; some are painters; some are bankers; some are light skinned, and some are dark skinned. The differences add to the beauty of the world. *[Add people figures to the flannel board.]* God told the people to take care of all that had been made. And God saw everything that had been made. How do you think God felt? Can we say it? "God saw that this was good." That's right. God saw that it was very good.

When God finished all this work, God rested.

What did you notice about the end of each day's work? God saw that it was good. God was happy about the work God was doing. We are happy that God has made a beautiful world for us and filled the world with so many different and good things. One of the songs in our hymnbook tells this story to music. *[Show the children the hymn "All Things Bright and Beautiful." It would be helpful to include this hymn as part of the worship service too.]*

**Prayer:** God, you have made a good world. Thank you for so many different things that make our world beautiful. Amen.

## You Can Count On It

**Purpose:** To identify God as dependable.
**Scripture:** Psalm 104:27–28.
**Materials:** Bible.

**Sermon:** It's important for us to know we can count on certain things to happen. We know that when we go to bed at night, we will get up the next day and it will be morning. All the time day follows night and night follows day. Even though the nights seem longer in the winter and the days seem longer in the summer, day follows night and night follows day.

We know that the seasons always come in the same order. There's summer, fall, winter, and spring. Every year it's the same. Winter never comes after spring, and summer never comes after fall. Sunday always comes after Saturday, and Monday always comes after Sunday.

What are some other things we count on to happen in order? *[If the children have difficulty thinking of things, make suggestions about trees that lose their leaves in winter or caterpillars that turn into butterflies.]*

What kind of babies do cats have? What about dogs? Do dogs ever have kittens? Do cats ever have puppies? We count on animals having baby animals just like themselves. We know when our pet gerbil has babies, we will have more gerbils. We won't have fish or rabbits or birds.

When we hear the story of God creating the world, we know that God created the world with a special order. God planned for things to follow one another in order. We also remember that God provided for all different parts of creation to be taken care of. God has promised us that the world will continue.

Do you know that the creation is still going on? It didn't stop way back at the beginning. There are new babies born all the time. They are new parts of God's creation. When you were born we knew that God's creation was still happening, and you were part of it. God has planned for new life to keep going. New trees and flowers and plants grow on the earth to provide food for all living creatures.

If we open the Bible to the middle, we will find the book of Psalms. The psalms are very old songs or hymns, kind of like the songs in our hymnbook. When we read some of Psalm 104 *[show these verses to the children]*, we hear that God made springs and rivers so every animal would have water to drink. God made grass to feed the cows and trees to hold the nests of the birds. God made mountains for the wild goats and food for the lions of the forest. God provides food for all things. God takes care of the creation.

Some of you may use the prayer "God is great. God is good. And we thank God for our food. For by God's hand we all are fed. Thank you God for daily bread." This prayer helps us remember that God has created the world and has given food for us and for all people.

God has made a promise to us and to all of creation.

What is a promise? What promises have your mom and dad made to you? What promises have you made? When people keep their promises to us, we can count on them. We can trust them. We can depend on them. When we keep our promises to someone else, that person counts on us and trusts us. We are dependable.

God has made a promise to us and to all of creation. God has promised that creation will keep going in a dependable way. For hundreds and thousands of years God has kept this promise. We can depend on God. We can trust God.

**Prayer:** God, it's so nice to know that you are keeping the world going. We have learned to depend on you for the seasons, for day and night, for everything. Thank you for being dependable and keeping your promises. Help us to be dependable too. Amen.

# It's My Job

**Purpose:** To describe our responsibility for caring for God's gift of creation.
**Scripture:** 1 Peter 4:10.
**Materials:** Goldfish in a fish bowl; a living plant.

**Sermon:** Today we are going to talk about jobs. You know, everybody has a job of some kind. Let's think about your house. What kinds of jobs do you do at your house? *[Let the children name some of their specific responsibilities such as making their beds, picking up their toys, dusting, folding laundry, setting or clearing the table, or caring for pets. As each child makes a contribution to the discussion, ask the other children how many of them do that job also.]*
I'm sure there are other jobs at your house that need to be done. Who cuts the grass? Who washes the windows? Who does the grocery shopping? Who takes care of the cars? Who cares for the flowers? *[Give the children time to answer these questions. If they help with these tasks, affirm their participation in the family.]* It takes lots of work by everyone to keep our homes neat and in working order.
In our church there are lots of jobs to be done too. Someone needs to take care of the grass in the summer and the parking lot in the winter; someone needs to keep the furniture dusted and the floors swept. Someone comes to church early on Sundays to open the doors for everyone else. Our teachers spend time during the week getting ready to teach class on Sunday. *[It would be helpful if you named some people in your congregation who do these tasks. You could have these people stand as you say their names.]* In this way our church is like our homes. It takes lots of people working together to keep the church neat and in working order. When we all help, the job gets done a lot faster and a lot better. Being part of the church means helping do the work of the church. What are some ways we help take care of our church? *[If the children hesitate, remind them that they pick up the trash in*

130

*their church school rooms after they finish a project, they clean up spills of paint, glue, or juice, they take care of church property when they help sweep their rooms or when they are careful with the hymnbooks, they put away supplies when they are finished using them.]*

When we are given a gift, we need to take care of the gift so it will last, just like we take care of our homes and our church. Suppose I gave you a goldfish for your birthday. *[Show the fish bowl with the goldfish.]* How would you take care of this fish? *[Remind the children that the fish needs to be fed every day. The water in the fish bowl must be kept clean, so it must be changed about once a week.]* What happens if we don't feed the fish?

Suppose I gave you a plant like this one. *[Show the children a plant such as a philodendron, geranium, or violet.]* How would you need to take care of this plant? *[The plant needs to be watered regularly. Sometimes it needs plant food or needs to be transplanted into a larger pot.]* If the plant isn't cared for, it will die.

God has given us a great and important gift, the world. It is our job to take care of the world. We do our job by putting trash in trash containers and not throwing it on the ground. We care for the world when we just admire wildflowers and don't pick them. We care for the birds when we put birdfeeders in our trees. What are some other ways we help take care of the world? *[Some of the children may know about recycling paper and cans. Others may mention planting flowers.]*

People are part of God's gift of creation too. When we help other people we are taking care of God's gift. When we bring food for the food basket and money for the offering and give away used clothes, we are helping to take care of others.

One of the reasons we know God loves us is because God gives us the gift of creation that includes our families, our homes, our church, and our friends. When we help take care of these things, we are showing we love God too.

**Prayer:** Thank you, God, for your many gifts, especially the gift of creation. Help us to remember that it is our job to help take care of this gift by working with others. Amen.

# D. Special Days

## Introduction *by Joseph H. Bragg, Jr.*
## Sermons *by Louise Bates Evans*

In addition to those high Sundays that the seasons of the church year bring, there are other special days that are celebrated as a part of congregational life. Many of these come in the fall of the year and thus are a part of the season of Pentecost.

Some congregations begin their church school classes in September with a renewed emphasis on Christian education. Several sermons in the section on "Discipleship" focus on growing and learning and thus lend themselves to use on this occasion.

Church loyalty is another emphasis that is often observed during September and October. The sermons under "The Church" will be appropriate at this time.

Stewardship is often a vital part of church life during the fall. The first two sermons of the "Discipleship" section will be helpful.

In late November, National Bible Week is observed. "The Bible, A Treasure Map" (Epiphany #6) and "Loving by the Rules" (Pentecost #15) can be used to focus on the gift of the Scriptures that is ours.

Peace Sunday comes in early December for some churches. Appropriate sermons for the moments with children are "The Armor of God" (Pentecost #20) and "How Sad the Ways of War!" (Pentecost #21), the last two sermons under "Discipleship."

This section titled "Special Days" addresses four important celebrations: World Communion Sunday, All Saints' Day, Reformation Sunday, and Thanksgiving Sunday. They can be times of great meaning in the worship life of the congregation. Use the sermons as a way of integrating the special children's moments into the experience of the whole.

## Together at the Table
### (World Communion Sunday)

**Purpose:** To create in children a feeling of being linked with Christians throughout the world.
**Scripture:** Romans 12:5.
**Materials:** A tray or basket of broken rice cakes.

**Sermon:** *[Place the tray or basket on the communion table to be shared at the end of the sermon. Gather the children around the communion table for the sermon.]*

Do you remember the story of the little train that thought he couldn't make it over the hill? He said, "I think I can, I think I can," until he finally made it over the hill. I would say he had a vision or a dream that he could get over the hill before he actually made it.

One minister, or evangelist as he was called, kept hearing Jesus' words, "Go into all the world and preach the gospel." The more he thought about this, the more he could see Christians in every country of the world. This image became so vivid to him that he could see everybody who heard the gospel telling another person. His slogan became, "Each one, win one for Christ." He went about teaching and preaching all over the world.

As more and more persons became Christians, Jesse Bader, the evangelist, had another vision. "Wouldn't it be wonderful," he thought, "if all Christians the world over would celebrate communion together? After all, we are all one body in Jesus, no matter how many of us there are."

Dr. Bader thought about this again and again. He knew this would not be an easy task because here in America some Christians call themselves Disciples, some Lutherans, some Catholics, some Presbyterians. Some Christians commune every Sunday, some once a month, and some once every three months. This problem becomes more complicated when we think about Christians in other parts of the world, where time zones, customs, and cultures are different. How

133

could all Christians commune together?

Dr. Bader had a vision and dream of a large communion table that wrapped around the world. There would be American Christians sitting with Australian, and African, and Indian, and Chinese. Christians from every part of the world would be communing together. Finally, the thought came to him, "We could have one day, twenty-four hours, when all Christians could participate in communion and celebrate being one body of Christians. We would all be part of the body of Christians and members one of another."

This wonderful dream was the beginning of World Communion Sunday. Today as we celebrate the day, we are going to remember that we are part of the body of Christ and that we are members with Christians around the world. Since we are members with Christians in Asia—China, Japan, Korea, and the Philippines—and they are members with us, we will share their bread—rice cakes. Jesse Bader's dream has come true once again. [Pass the tray of broken rice cakes.]

**Prayer:** Heavenly Father, we thank you for Jesse Bader, who had a dream that Christians around the world could celebrate their oneness in Jesus. Give us dreams that show us how to live for Jesus and for each other. Amen.

# In Their Footsteps
## (All Saints' Day)

**Purpose:** To enable children to recognize and celebrate the lives of persons who are dedicated Christians.
**Scripture:** Hebrews 11:1–2; 12:1–2.
**Materials:** None.

**Sermon:** All of us know that our nation sets aside special days like Mother's Day and Father's Day. On those days we show our appreciation to our parents for the love and care they have given us.

The church also has special days, and one of these is All Saints' Day. Like Mother's Day and Father's Day, this is a day when we recognize and celebrate the lives of the saints.

Perhaps I am getting ahead of my story because I am not sure you know who saints are and how you can recognize them.

The Bible tells us that we are surrounded by a great cloud of witnesses—persons who lived their lives so that people could see that they loved God. These people are saints.

We can name some saints from Bible times. I'll start with Abraham, Moses, and Joseph from the Old Testament and from the New Testament, Mary, the mother of Jesus, the widow who gave all she had to others, and the apostle Peter. Surely these were saints. You can name many more if you take time to think about it.

We also have a couple of saints that you all know—St. Nicholas and St. Valentine. What makes all of these people saints?

Saints are persons who love God and are strong enough to love their neighbors as themselves. Saints are heroes and heroines of the church. They are models in whose footsteps we follow. The present-day saints are everyday people. They are Mother Teresa, friend of the dying in India, and Samantha Smith, the little peace ambassador. But they are also the doctors, nurses, teachers, firemen, our parents, and the old

135

pioneers of our congregations.

We celebrate their lives because they are an inspiration to us. Saints lead the way. They break new ground. They set an example for us to live by.

Sometimes it is not easy to follow in their footsteps. I remember once trying to follow in someone's footsteps. It was the winter that I was seven years old, and we woke up to the deepest snow I had ever seen. The snow was almost up to my knees. My grandmother assured me that I could make the short trip to school if I stepped in the tracks, the footsteps, that adults had made along the way. I followed those tracks, stepping, jumping, leaping, and sometimes falling because the adult's legs were longer than mine. But the journey was easier because someone had gone before me, leaving their tracks for me to follow. And so we celebrate the lives of saints, persons who love God and show us how to love each other.

There is a song that the church has sung for a long time: "When the saints go marching in, I want to be in that number." We can be in the number if we say to ourselves, "A saint is a responsible person, someone just like you and me, who with God helps the world take care of itself."

**Prayer:** Dear God, I want to be a saint. Help me to live my life so that people will know that I love you and that I want to make this a caring world. Amen.

# A New Day in the Church
## (Reformation Sunday)

**Purpose:** To show appreciation for persons who risked the loss of friendship because they cared greatly about the church.
**Scripture:** Matthew 21:13a.
**Materials:** None.

**Sermon:** Have you ever found yourself doing things that you thought were wrong just because your friends would laugh and call you names if you didn't? Sometimes we see situations that we think are wrong. We may see people who hurt others or who are unkind to people who are different. Sometimes we may see our friends take things that belong to others and bully them. Many times we turn our heads to avoid being involved. It is never easy to take a stand for what you believe is right if others disagree. Most of the time we just want to fit in with the crowd.

Jesus was not afraid to take a stand or speak out for what he believed was right. Jesus felt strongly about the church. He knew that the Old Testament said that the church should be called a house of prayer. Jesus was very upset by what he saw: The house of prayer had become a marketplace. How could that be? On one occasion, Jesus became so upset that he stormed into the temple, overturning tables, scattering coins everywhere, and releasing the doves that were in their cages. The people going in and out of the temple were surprised because they had become accustomed to making purchases at the temple. They did not agree with Jesus, but Jesus stood for what he believed. Because of Jesus' actions, the church was reformed or made new.

Many years later another man, Martin Luther, also believed that the church should be called a house of prayer. By this time the church had forgotten many of the teachings of Jesus. Once again, the church had become a marketplace. This time people could buy "indulgences" or certificates that

137

said "You are forgiven." The more money a person had, the more of these indulgences he or she could buy. Martin Luther was saddened by this church practice. He believed that forgiveness is a gift of God that cannot be bought or sold. Martin Luther spoke out for what he believed. He had the courage to take his stand because the Bible tells the story of Jesus in the temple and how he took a stand.

It is never easy to take a stand for what you think is right if others around you disagree. Luther expected the local people and the church to disagree with him, but instead many people supported his new ideas. Some, of course, did not want to change the ways to which they had been accustomed. Eventually, because he was willing to risk being unpopular, more people accepted his new ideas and a new day began in the church. Reformation Sunday is the celebration of that time when the church was reformed—improved or made new.

If we take Jesus' message seriously, the church can experience a new day again and again. The church can be a house of prayer, where we pray for persons in distress, those who are homeless and less fortunate than ourselves. We can experience a new day by welcoming the stranger in our midst and being willing to take risks for what we believe is right.

**Prayer:** Dear God, we thank you for Jesus and Martin Luther, who remembered that your house shall be called a house of prayer. Help us to be strong enough to risk taking a stand for what is right. Amen.

## Thanks—Giving
### (Thanksgiving Sunday)

**Purpose:** To communicate a sense of responsibility to share the gifts we receive from God.
**Scripture:** Luke 12:48b.
**Materials:** None.

**Sermon:** Do you know what Sunday this is? Today is Thanksgiving Sunday. What comes to your mind when you think of Thanksgiving? Do you think of Thanksgiving dinner, turkey and all the trimmings? Or do you think of the first Thanksgiving with the Pilgrims and Indians sharing a meal? Americans called that celebration the first Thanksgiving, but Thanksgiving is a religious celebration and goes back to our foreparents in the Old Testament. This was a time when the Jewish people thanked God for the harvest, the bountiful crop of fruits and vegetables.

As you listen to a story of two men and their harvest, try to put yourself in their place and tell me which one expressed Thanksgiving.

According to the Book of Ruth in the Old Testament, there was a farmer named Boaz, who had vast fields of grain. When it came time to harvest the grain, he instructed the workers to make one cutting of the field. All of the grain left around the edges of the field could be gathered by the poor persons—the homeless and the widows—so that they, too, would have food to eat.

The New Testament tells us of another man who was also a prosperous farmer. His fields of grain reached far and wide. One day he realized that this was the biggest and best harvest he had ever had. So he tore down his old barn and built new and larger barns to hold all the grain. He felt so good about himself! "Ah," he said, "now I am a wealthy man. I can retire and live off my profits." He thought only of himself.

I imagine each thought he was thankful, but which man

had thanksgiving in his heart? Which man was truly thankful? *[Let the children express their ideas.]*

Thanksgiving requires that in our thankfulness we share the gifts God has given us. As we say thank you to God we are required to share with others less fortunate than ourselves. For us, this might include people in our own neighborhoods or children in our own schools. It would include persons who are homeless, unemployed, or victims of disasters. There are many people and groups that our church is aware of whom we help as a way of expressing our thankfulness. Our offerings on this Sunday reflect our spirit of thanksgiving. Our Thanksgiving responsibility, then, is to say thank you and to share generously what we have been given.

**Prayer:** Dear God, on this Thanksgiving Sunday, we thank you for the gifts you have given us. Help us to show our love for you and each other by sharing our blessings with others. Amen.

# Index to Scriptures

| | |
|---|---|
| Luke 1:26–33 | Advent/Christmas #2 |
| 1:46–55 | Advent/Christmas #3 |
| 2:1–20 | Advent/Christmas #5 |
| 2:8–14 | Advent/Christmas #4 |
| 2:41–51 | Easter #5 |
| 4:1–14 | Epiphany #3 |
| 6:12–16 | Epiphany #4 |
| 9:51–58 | Pentecost #11 |
| 10:25–37 | Epiphany #8 |
| 10:38–41 | Pentecost #13 |
| 12:16–21 | Pentecost #8 |
| 12:48b | Pentecost #28 |
| 14:1–6 | Pentecost #15 |
| 15:11–32 | Easter #3 |
| 19:2–9 | Lent #2 |
| | |
| John 6:5–14 | Pentecost #4 |
| 13:15 | Pentecost #3 |
| 15:9–17 | Easter #4 |
| 17:20–21 | Pentecost #6 |
| | |
| Acts 2:1-4a | Pentecost #1 |
| Romans 12:5 | Pentecost #25 |
| 2 Corinthians 5:18 | Pentecost #7 |
| Galatians 3:28 | Epiphany #9 |
| Ephesians 2:19 | Pentecost #2 |
| 6:10–20 | Pentecost #20 |
| Hebrews 11:1–2; 12:1–2 | Pentecost #26 |
| 1 Peter 4:10 | Pentecost #24 |

# Contributors

**Sue Amyx** is an ordained minister of the Christian Church (Disciples of Christ) who serves the Christian Church in Allenville, Illinois. Before moving to the Allenville church, she served eight-and-a-half years as associate minister at First Christian Church in Manhattan, Kansas. She received her undergraduate degree from Eureka College and earned her Master of Divinity and Doctor of Ministry degrees from Brite Divinity School at Texas Christian University. She is a curriculum writer and educational consultant. She is president of the Association of Christian Church Educators.

**Jim Benton** is pastor of First Christian Church (Disciples of Christ) in Stuttgart, Arkansas. His interest in children and worship has guided his work in the church for many years. It led to the creation of Welcome to Worship (a course to prepare first graders and their parents for worship), a unique yearlong Preparation for Christian Adulthood (preparing older children and families for baptism), dozens of workshops to prepare adults for worship with children, and hundreds of unique moments with children in worship.

**Dixie Holt Deen** is an ordained minister of the Christian Church (Disciples of Christ). She holds a Bachelor of Arts degree from Texas Christian University, Fort Worth, and a Master of Religious Education from Brite Divinity School of Texas Christian University.

**Louise Bates Evans** is Director of Family and Children's Ministries in the Department of Christian Education in the Division of Homeland Ministries of the Christian Church (Disciples of Christ). She serves the regions and congregations by training leaders who work with families and children and by developing programs that enable these ministries. Prior to coming to this position, Louise was professor of family studies at Purdue University and Virginia Polytechnic Institute. She received the doctorate in education from Indiana University and the master's and bachelor's degrees in child development and family life from Purdue University. Louise is married to Rev. Lorenzo J. Evans and is the mother of young adult children.

**R. Larry Hallett** is pastor of Pacific Beach Christian Church in San Diego, California. He is a graduate of Indiana University and the School of Theology at Claremont, California. Prior to going to San Diego, he was Director of Merchandising for Christian Board of Publication. During seminary he served First Christian Church in Santa Monica, and Hollydale Christian Church in South Gate, California.

**Janet Hellner-Burris** enjoys working with children of all ages as the associate pastor of First Christian Church in Minneapolis. She began thinking about professional ministry while teaching the Bible to inner city children in her home congregation in Washington, D.C. She received her Master of Divinity degree from Princeton Theological Seminary. For inspiration, she goes on long walks with her husband, Steve, their daughter, Katie, and their dog, Buffy.

**John T. Hinant** and his wife, Eleyce, are the parents of four and the grandparents of four. He is a Hoosier who spent ten years of his ministry at the National City Christian Church in Washington, D.C., where he directed a Headstart center. The past twenty years he has been minister of Christian education and mission at Northwood Christian Church in Indianapolis. He received his formal education at Indiana University, The Institute for Child Study at the University of Maryland, Brite College of the Bible at Texas Christian University, and Christian Theological Seminary in Indianapolis. He holds a Bachelor of Arts degree in philosophy and three graduate professional degrees.

**Patrice L. Rosner** is an editor at Christian Board of Publication working primarily on materials for children's ministries. She has edited curriculum resources for church school classes for children ages two through eleven, vacation church school for children in nursery through sixth grade, and church membership classes for older elementary children through adults. In her congregation Patrice has worked with children ages 2-5 in a music program and in extended session during worship, taught church school, led teacher training events, and serves as the chairperson of the Christian education committee. Her seven-year-old daughter, Kara, helps keep her in touch with children.